ENTREPRENEUR BOOT CAMP

by

ARNOLD SANOW

GIRARD A. PERONE

KENDALL/HUNT PUBLISHING COMPANY
4050 Westmark Drive Dubuque, Iowa 52002

Books and Cassettes by Jerry Perone

Lawsuits and Asset Protection

Simply Your Cash Flow Analysis

Asset Protection Planning

How To Structure Your Business and Personal Affairs

The Corporation Manual

How To Bullet Proof Your Corporation

Profits, Privacy, Protection

Books and Cassettes by Arnold Sanow

Marketing Boot Camp

Dazzle Your Customer . . . You're the Key to Effective Customer Service

Marketing Professional Services

Winning Presentation Skills

Communicate Like a Pro

Quantity Discounts Available for
Entrepreneur Boot Camp
Call 1-800-228-0810

Library of Congress Catalog Card Number: 94-74573

ISBN 0-7872-0253-3

Printed in the United States of America
10 9 8 7 6 5 4 3 2 1

Dedicated to the successful start-up, continuing growth and ultimate success of our clients.

Table of Contents

A Word About "Entrepreneur Boot Camp"

Welcome to Boot Camp. This book is one in a series designed to help you achieve the success you deserve. The Boot Camp books cover a wide range of topics in the areas of business and finance.

The Boot Camp books provide you with the information and skill that will help you be successful. Each book is based on a simple formula for success—you can do it. This formula will help you assess your skills, talents and resources, then follow a pattern of time-tested steps which lead you to the achievement of your goals.

Like a battle plan, each book shows you how to get to where you want to go, what it will take to get there, and how to steer around the obstacles you will face along the way.

The Boot Camp books are easy to read, understandable and free of textbook drabness and jargon. The material is presented in a format that allows you to either read it cover to cover or use it for quick reference and reminders.

Throughout each book, you will find highlighted quotations, easy-to-locate information and immensely important advice from leaders in the field.

At the end of each book, you will find a kit of important documents to get you started and a list of resources to help you further your understanding of the task at hand.

We wish you the greatest success. We are certain that the "Entrepreneur Boot Camp" will give you the knowledge and the confidence to achieve the American Dream.

> *"The business of America is business."*
>
> CALVIN COOLIDGE

Introduction

The opportunity to start your own business has never been greater than it is today. Worldwide markets are opening, and entrepreneurs of all descriptions are discovering that they can indeed be successful in their own ventures.

There are now over 20 million small non-farm businesses in America. Last year there were a record 702,000 corporations formed. Small businesses have been increasing at the rate of over 6% per year.

Small businesses now contribute over 60% of the jobs in the U.S. and are responsible for 50% of the gross domestic product.

Faced with poor job prospects, more and more middle-aged victims of the downsizing war in the U.S. are going out on their own rather then be told time and time again, "We will keep your resume on file." Women are returning to the workforce with their own businesses. Military veterans, minorities, teenagers, the handicapped and many other subgroups are opting for the independence, tax advantages and control of entrepreneurship.

The decision to go into business for yourself must be your own decision. In addition, it must be a *business* decision, following months of planning, discussion and contemplation. It must not be based on impulse, whim or emotional fervor. It's an important, strategic life decision, one that will affect your family, your finances and your outlook on life.

We are enthusiastic about what this book can do for you, and we hope that you find it to be an important first step and valuable tool in guiding you to success. We have found that most entrepreneurs are made, not born. So let's get started by discussing in Chapter One what are your chances of success.

JERRY PERONE and ARNOLD SANOW

Biographies

Jerry Perone, BS and MBA, is president of the National Management Center, Inc., a nationwide business and financial consulting firm. He has helped establish dozens of corporations, partnerships and Limited Liability Companies across the US. Prior to starting his own business, Jerry spent 24 years in corporate America. Serving as a senior member of the IBM Corporation, he was involved with many corporate start-up ventures. He knows how to put together a solid business plan and how to make it profitable. Jerry has helped both small and large businesses meet their financial goals. He is the author of *Wealth: How to Make It, How to Keep It*, due out in 1995. Jerry is a frequent guest on television and in the print media. He is also an adjunct professor at Howard University and a member of the International Executive Service Corps and the Project Management Institute. Jerry's address is 6701 Democracy Boulevard, Suite 300, Bethesda, MD 20817. His phone number is 301-590-0710.

Arnold Sanow, MBA, is president of the Business Source, Inc., a business development and training company. He consults with businesses from start-ups to those in the Fortune 500 companies. In addition, he has given over 2,000 paid presentations and training programs on various business topics throughout the USA and overseas. He has appeared on numerous television and radio shows, such as CBS Evening News with Dan Rather, Nations Business, Smart Money, and Worldnet, and has been featured in such magazines and newspapers as *Entrepreneur Magazine, USA Today* and the *Washington Times.* He is co-author of the best selling books, *You Can Start Your Own Business* and *Marketing Boot Camp*. In addition, he is the former host of the radio show, "It's Your Business," and a regular columnist for the Washington Business Advisor. He has been the national small-business spokesperson for AT&T's 800 number and Intuit's Quick-Books software. He is an adjunct professor at Georgetown University. Arnold's address is 2810 Glade Vale Way, Vienna, VA 22181. His phone number is 703-255-3133.

CHAPTER ONE

What Are My Chances For Success?

Chapter Chart

The line between success and failure is usually a small one. Running a business is like running a race. In many cases the difference between first and second place is usually as small as 1/100 of a second. The person with the knowledge, skills, abilities and above all the extra effort is the one who will succeed in his or her own business. This chapter will review the following:

- How to develop an action plan to make sure you make your dreams come true.
- How to handle the disappointments that will come along.
- The factors that are essential to running any successful business and why learning from others and copying success is one of your best strategies.
- The three key ingredients that you must have to be successful.

Success Is Up To You

There are three qualities you must have to ultimately be successful in your own business. These are:

1. Awareness—You must know and understand every ingredient of your business. It's not enough to have the technical expertise; you must also be versed in the financial, marketing, man-

agement, and day-to-day concerns that ultimately determine success or failure. *Entrepreneur Boot Camp* and *Marketing Boot Camp* will help you become aware of the key elements essential to running a small business.

2. Commitment—Once you learn the ingredients essential to success, you must make a commitment to do something about it. There are many people around who have the knowledge, skills and abilities to be successful, but they have never taken *action* to make their dreams come true.
3. Discipline—You must be obsessive in reaching your goals. Starting and operating a business is not just a 9-to-5 job. You must set a regular routine and stick to it. For example, 90% of the people who go on diets gain their weight back in a short time. If they stuck to a regular routine and did not deviate, they could keep their weight off indefinitely. To make your business work, you too must discipline yourself and get into the habit of success.

TAKE ACTION!!!

> *"What we think or what we know or what we believe is, in the end, of little consequence. The only consequence is what we do."*
>
> JOHN RUSKIN

In order to start your own business, you must take action. Reading and studying alone will not help you achieve your goals. Action of some form or another is the answer to all your problems and the realization of all your goals. We, therefore, would like to provide you with this Action Planner.

Make copies of this page, write out your ideas, thoughts, and action items and see how quickly good things will come to you.

Action Planner

	What I've Learned	The Actions I Will Take	Date to Start	Date to Complete
1				
2				
3				
4				
5				
6				
7				
8				
9				
10				
11				
12				
13				
14				

LEARN FROM OTHERS

"Sow the same seeds and you'll reap the same rewards." In other words, produce the same results that successful people produce, and you too will be successful.

You can increase the chances of business success by learning from the experiences of the others who have gone before you. Few business failures stem from a single cause. One cause may predominate, but inadequate responses to several interrelated factors typically lead to a company's failure. Since the Industrial Revolution, there have been literally hundreds of millions of businesses—businesses that have thrived, businesses that have never been able to get off the ground. It's hard to imagine a new, undiscovered cause for failure in the 1990s and beyond. You should study businesses in the market that you plan to enter. You should look at the characteristics that made successful businesses successful. In addition, you should be sure to look at the characteristics that caused failed businesses to fail.

Many causes of failure have already been documented. Generally, these causes fall into two categories—external factors and internal factors.

EXTERNAL FACTORS

- Local or regional recession
- Unexpected loss of a major supplier
- Unexpected loss of a major customer
- A strike, fire, natural disaster
- New competitors entering the marketplace

INTERNAL FACTORS

- Inadequate accounting and control systems
- Inadequate capital
- Lack of management expertise
- Poor financial management and overpayment of taxes
- Growth cannot keep pace with financing
- Poor cash flow management

WHAT IS A BUSINESS FAILURE?

If you are worried about failing, maybe you shouldn't go into business in the first place. Fear will affect your decisions. But just in case, a word to the wise may be sufficient about failure. At the very onset of your business planning, you should decide what would have to happen to constitute failure. Or conversely, what results would define business success? Given enough time (decades for some, centuries for others) all businesses will fail and go out of business.

For 75 years Pan American Airlines was THE premier airline in America. It officially went out of business in 1992. In 1993 the Pan Am logo was sold at auction for an undisclosed amount.

Drexel Burnham, a first class Wall Street investment banking firm for almost a century, closed its doors in the late eighties. IBM was a model of business and management for over 50 years. Since 1988, IBM has seen profits disappear that resulted in a reduction of force by close to 300,000 professionals and blue collar employees worldwide.

Were these examples cases of business failures? Possibly. But thousands upon thousands of people made huge amounts of money from these companies during their heydays. These businesses employed millions of people, many still living off their pensions.

Before you start your new business, take a few moments to decide under what conditions you would consider your venture to be a failure. If you only make $50,000 per year, would you be a failure? What about $10,000? Maybe if you lose all the capital that you put up to start the business, that would be failure.

We are not sure. This is a personal decision for you alone to figure out. We feel that there is no such thing as a business failure. There are just delays in your business's success. If things get bad, pull back, regroup, get some more capital and go for it!

YOUR CHANCE OF SUCCESS

What we notice in our consulting practice is that successful entrepreneurs do not blame external factors or internal factors. They grab full responsibility with both hands and get on the road to success. The buck stops with you. When entrepreneurs prepare to take full responsibilty for their business, it seems they do a far better job with the planning phase. Since there are no outs, they tend to think through every detail, every possibility for something to go wrong, and plan around these possibilities.

Your chances of being successful will be near 100% if you follow the three major rules presented in this chapter.

- First, before you decide that you have failed, decide what failure is.
- Second, accept full responsibility for the business. Take no prisoners.
- Third, take action.

So, let's get going with your business.

CHAPTER TWO

Do You Have What It Takes?

"Everything comes to him who hustles while he waits."
THOMAS ALVA EDISON

Chapter Chart

Do you want to succeed as a business owner, or entrepreneur? This chapter explains what an entrepreneur is and what kind of person finds success and fulfillment in starting his or her **own business.**

- Webster's dictionary defines an entrepreneur as "one who organizes, manages and assumes the risks of a business or enterprise."
- Research shows that successful entrepreneurs are upbeat, goal-oriented, comfortable with taking risks, organized, committed, energetic, adaptable, authoritative, responsible, self-aware and persevering.
- Common weaknesses of entrepreneurs include poor judgment, permitting interruptions and working without a well-thought-out plan.

You can test your business potential by taking the following quiz. Your answers will help you judge whether you have the personality, skills and drive to be your own boss.

TEST YOUR BUSINESS POTENTIAL

Rate each question on a 1 to 5 scale. 1 = never or no, and 5 = always or yes.

Do you have experience in the business you want to go into? _____

The most successful entrepreneurs have either grown up in the business they're going into or worked for someone else.

Do you spend your money wisely? _____

Successful entrepreneurs tend to keep their overhead low, but invest in the "tools" that will make them successful.

Are you reliable? _____

Successful entrepreneurs do what they say they are going to do, do it when they say they are going to do it, do it right the first time and get it done on time.

Is your personal appearance the best it can be? _____

Successful entrepreneurs dress and make the effort to look like someone their customers would trust and like.

Are your home and office organized, neat and clean? _____

Successful entrepreneurs have a clean, neat and organized operation.

Do you have an upbeat attitude most of the time? _____

Do you see the good, beautiful, and optimistic side, or are you pessimistic and see the down side of everything?

Do you have a sincere passion for the business you want to go into? _____

The most successful entrepreneurs live by the motto, "Do what you love and the money will follow."

Do you have a high energy level? _____

As you'll find in running a successful business, you probably won't be too successful if you only put in a 9-to-5 day. Most entrepreneurs work 10 to 12 hours a day and more!

Do you have persistence? _____

Walt Disney had 302 bank refusals before he got funding. Would you have stuck it out?

Are you creative? _____

To be competitive in the 1990s and beyond you need to be open-minded and innovative.

Do you have self discipline? _____

You're now in an unstructured job role. No one tells you when to get up, to go to work or what to do. Can you set your own routine?

Do you have a mentor or a coach? _____

Successful entrepreneurs attach themselves to experts in the field they want to go into. This saves time and money and helps to avoid mistakes.

Do you have the ability to make decisions? _____

Successful entrepreneurs tend to make decisions quickly and change their minds slowly. In other words, they give their decisions a chance to work before discarding them.

Are you willing to consult with others during start-up and beyond? _____

Business is risky at best. You can reduce the risks by getting advice from your accountant, lawyer, banker and business consultant.

Do you set goals? _____

To succeed you must have written goals that are specific, measurable, acceptable and realistic and have a time frame.

Scoring

65–75 = successful entrepreneur

55–64 = average entrepreneur

45–54 = borderline entrepreneur

44 and under = keep your job

Whatever your score, don't become discouraged. The purpose of this self test is for you to be aware of the characteristics and traits of successful entrepreneurs and what you must do to succeed. If your score is low, you can take action to compensate. For example, you might hire outside consultants or a person who is an expert in the field of your business.

Going into business for yourself remains one of the most exciting, fulfilling and challenging things you can ever do. It could also be one of the most risky and difficult. But if you are committed to making your business work and take into account the pitfalls that may lie ahead, you, too, can join the ranks of those who have turned their business dreams into reality.

There are many success stories in the world of small business.

> Julie, a single mother and high school dropout with three children, received some child support. She worked as a chef's assistant in a neighborhood restaurant. She was responsible for planning the menus and supervising the staff in the chef's absence. Then the restaurant was sold and Julie was unemployed.
>
> Aware of Julie's plight, a former customer asked if she'd like to cater a brunch the following weekend. Julie accepted. Julie overcame her anxiety about the new opportunity, and she enjoyed planning, cooking and being in charge. The brunch went very well—and it led to a few more catering jobs. Julie soon knew she had found what she wanted to do. She decided to go into business for herself.
>
> Julie distributed fliers and waited for the jobs to roll in. But the phone was depressingly silent and bills began to pile up. Although Julie had discovered the satisfaction of being her own boss, she needed something more to make her business successful.
>
> Then Julie had an idea. She remembered the customers who had appreciated her service. How could she get their business again? What if she set up a catering service that delivered? She could cater private lunches and dinners for her old customers and business lunches for offices in the area. She assembled a suitable crew of her former workmates. She contacted offices and residences in the neighborhood.
>
> She did so well she amazed herself. In a few weeks, business was booming. Without a high school diploma or special training, Julie was now a successful business owner—her own boss as well as the boss of others. And she had created a better life for herself and her family.

PREPARE TO AMAZE YOURSELF

People like Julie, with little more than a good idea and a few friends to help, often amaze themselves. The energy that results from a focused, concentrated effort in making a successful business venture enables them to accomplish more than they ever did at a job.

Entrepreneurs are often the toughest bosses of all. The late-night and weekend hours they dreaded when working for someone else become less work and more challenge.

HOW DO YOU MATCH UP?

> *"If entrepreneurs are distinguished by anything, it is by the simple fact that they act on thoughts most everyone at one time or another has had."*
>
> THOMAS JONES, *ENTREPRENEURISM*

In recent years, much attention has been paid to whether entrepreneurs are made or born. Research indicates that heredity, educational background, work values, family traits and environmental circumstances have a profound influence on an individual's decision to become a business owner. Since we have worked with over 500 business owners in more than 50 lines of work, we have come to know and appreciate the traits and values shared by successful entrepreneurs. Some of their common strengths appear below.

Common Strength of Entrepreneurs

Upbeat—Are positive and open to new possibilities.

Goal-Oriented—Have the ability to enlist others around them in pursuit of goals.

Reward-Seeking—Need to be visibly rewarded for their creativity and risk taking.

Comfortable with Risk—Thrive on a certain degree of risk.

Organized—Create systems that accomplish the task at hand.

Committed—Have a "whatever it takes" attitude.

Energetic—Have high energy and get sick far less often than normal.

Adaptable—Are able to modify their behavior to meet changing conditions.

Authoritative—Are self-assured and willing to take charge.

Believable—Appear to be genuine people.

Responsible—Recognize that they control their own destiny.

Self-Aware—Have an understanding of what they do well and what they don't do well.

Persevering—Are willing to keep going when most people would give up.

Each of the strengths shared by entrepreneurs also has its down side. For example, the business owner committed to working hard may abandon the family and friends that serve as an essential part of his or her support system. Or an excessively organized entrepreneur may waste valuable time fine-tuning procedures—time that could be better spent generating new business.

What Steps Do I Take To Start Up My Business?

1. Complete business plan
2. Locate adequate office space
3. Check zoning regulations
4. Determine your business type
5. Select and register your business name
6. Obtain and file needed licenses, permits and registrations
7. Design and print your brochures, letters and flyers
8. Set up your bookkeeping and accounting system
9. Get needed equipment and supplies
10. Set up your telephone service
11. Set up your mail service
12. Establish a separate business bank account line of credit
13. Get insurance
14. Establish a work schedule
15. Get a mentor/coach . . . model . . . copy success

Paul Breaux, a real estate developer in North Carolina put it this way:

> "I was very, very poor, and I had that drive, that focus on—I hate to say financial success, because as we all know now, success isn't measured in numbers of dollars. That has nothing to do with it. Money is a dissatisfier. If you have it, it won't make you happy. If you don't have it, then it can make you unhappy. So it is a negative as far as motivation. What I wanted to do was show myself that someone can come out of meager means—my father left my family when I was 12 years old, so I didn't have a lot of male influence in my life. I felt abandoned. I think that is perfectly normal. I felt like I had to come out of the situation better than I had been left. So I wanted to prove, not only to myself, but to prove to all of my friends, that I was more than I appeared to be. I was more than cheap, ratty, little apartments, and hot dogs and beans. I was different than that. That just happened to be the circumstance that I was in at the time.
>
> "The most important step in any journey is the **first** step. Make sure you are dedicated to seeing it through. Focus on the idea that you will be successful. Tell yourself that you will be successful and do all of those things that make you achieve your goals. This is the most important thing besides having drive. Know where you are going. Be a goal setter. Live by your goals—short-term goals and long-term goals. But know where you are going, and don't take advantage of opportunities that don't lead you toward your goal. It's easy to get side-tracked in business and opportunities in life, but if it is not leading you toward your goal, then forget it."

Common Weaknesses of Entrepreneurs

Establish unrealistic time frames—Seek to achieve challenging goals quickly, and often underestimate the time and resources that will be necessary to achieve them.

Attempt to accomplish too much alone—Do not sufficiently delegate authority, tasks or responsibilities to subordinates. Also, many maintain hidden agendas that they attempt to accomplish by themselves.

Tolerate interruptions—Leave themselves wide open to interruption. The biggest culprits here are the telephone and the unscheduled appointment.

Work without a plan—Prepare an extensive plan at the start of a business, and then toss it in a file and forget about it. They tend to have an impulsive management style that can lead them in circles.

Do not do enough homework—Proceed into untested waters without sufficiently researching the prevailing environment. This can be a fatal mistake. The more preparation made in the initial steps of any venture, the easier it is in the long run.

CHAPTER THREE

The 30 Most Frequently Asked Questions—And Their Answers

For those people who want answers to their questions immediately, we have decided to put this list of the 30 most frequently asked questions about small businesses right up front in the book. We hope you will still read the remainder of the book, but here, thanks to some help by the Small Business Administration (SBA) Answer Desk, are answers to some of the most nagging questions.

1. Do I have what it takes to own/manage a small business?

   You will be your own most important employee, so an objective appraisal of your strengths and weaknesses is essential. Some questions to ask yourself are: Am I a self starter? How well do I get along with a variety of personalities? How good am I at making decisions? Do I have the physical and emotional stamina to run a business? How well do I plan and organize? Is my attitude and drive strong enough to keep myself motivated? How will the business affect my family?

2. What business should I choose?

   Usually, the best business for you is the one in which you are most skilled and interested in. Most important, do what you love and the money will follow. As you review your options, you may wish to consult local experts and businesspeople about the growth potential of various businesses in your area. Matching your background with the local market will increase your chance of success.

3. What is a business plan and why do I need one?

   The business plan answers two questions, "Where am I going?" and "How am I getting there?" A business plan precisely defines your business, identifies your goals and serves as your firm's resume. Its basic components include a current and pro-forma balance sheet, an income statement and a cash flow analysis. It helps you allocate resources properly, handle unforeseen complications and make the right decisions. Because it provides specific and organized information about your company and how you will repay borrowed money, a good business plan is a crucial part of any loan package. Additionally, it can tell your sales personnel, suppliers and others about your operations and goals.

4. Why do I need to define my business in detail?

   It may seem silly to ask yourself, "What business am I really in?", but some owner-managers have gone broke because they never answered that question. One watch store owner realized that most of his income came from repairing watches while most of his money was tied up in his inventory of watches. By "focusing" on the repair business and discarding his sales operations, he dramatically increased his profits.

5. What legal aspects do I need to consider?

   Licenses required, zoning laws and other regulations vary from business to business and from state to state. Your local SBA office and/or Chamber of Commerce will provide you with general information, but you will need to consult your attorney for advice specific to your enterprise and area. You also must decide about your form of organization (corporation, partnership or sole proprietorship) or tax status (e.g., should you opt for a Subchapter "S" status?).

6. What do I need to succeed in a business?

   There are five basics of success in small business:

   - Sound management practices
   - Industry experience

- Technical support
- Planning ability
- "Focused" goals

Few people start a business with all of these bases covered. Honestly assess your own experience and skills; then look for partners or key employees to compensate for your deficiencies.

7. Would a partner(s) make it easier to be successful?

   A business partner does not guarantee success. If you require additional management skills or start-up capital, engaging a partner may be your best decision. Personality and character, as well as ability to give technical or financial assistance, determine the ultimate success of a partnership.

8. How can I find qualified employees?

   Choose your employees carefully. Decide beforehand what you want them to do. Be specific. You may need flexible employees who can shift from task to task as required. Interview and screen applicants with care. Remember, good questions lead to good answers—the more you learn about each applicant's experience and skills, the better prepared you are to make your decision.

9. How do I set wage levels?

   Wage levels are calculated using the criteria of position importance and skill required. Consult your trade association and accountant to learn the most current practices, cost ratios and profit margins in your business field. While there is a minimum wage set by federal law for most jobs, the actual wage paid is entirely between you and your prospective employee.

10. What other financial responsibilities do I have for employees?

    You must withhold federal and state income taxes, contribute to unemployment and workers compensation systems, and match Social Security holdings. You may also wish to inquire about key employee life or disability insurance. Because laws on these matters vary from state to state, you probably should consult local information sources and/or SBA offices.

11. What kind of security measures must I take?

    Crimes ranging from armed robbery to embezzlement can destroy even the best businesses. You should install a good physical security system. Just as important, you must establish policies and safeguards to ensure awareness and honesty among your personnel. Because computer systems can be used to defraud as well as keep records, you should check into a computer security program. Consider taking seminars on how to spot and deter shoplifting and how to handle cash and merchandise; it is time and money well spent. Finally, careful screening when hiring can be your best ally against crime.

12. Should I hire family members to work for me?

    Frequently, family members of the owner "help out" in the business. For some small business owners it is a rewarding experience; for others it can cause irreparable damage. Carefully consider their loyalty and respect for you as the owner-manager. Can you keep your family and business decisions separate?

13. Do I need a computer?

    Small business today faces growing inventory requirements, increased customer expectations, rising costs and intense competition. Computers can provide information that leads to better returns on investment. At the same time, they help you cope with the many other pressures of your business. Computers are not cure-alls, however, and considerable care should be given to:

    - Deciding if you need one, and
    - Selecting the best computer system for your business.

14. How much money do I need to get started?

    Once you have taken care of your building and equipment needs you also must have enough money on hand to cover operating expenses for at least a year. These expenses include your salary as the owner and money to repay your loans. One of the leading causes of business failure is insufficient start-up capital. Consequently, you should work closely with your accountant to estimate your cash flow needs.

15. What are the alternatives in financing a business?

    Committing your own funds is often the first financing step. It is certainly the best indicator of how serious you are about your business. Risking your own money gives confidence for others to invest in your business. You may want to consider a partner for additional financing. Banks are an obvious source of funds. Other loan sources include commercial finance companies, venture capital firms, local development companies and life insurance companies. Trade credit, selling stock and equipment leasing offer alternatives to borrowing. Leasing, for example, can be an advantage because it does not tie up your cash. Ask your local SBA office for information about these various sources.

16. What do I have to do to get a loan?

    Initially, the lender will ask three questions:

    - How will you use the loan?
    - How much do you need to borrow?
    - How will you repay the loan?

    When you apply for the loan, you must provide projected financial statements and a cohesive, clear business plan which supplies the name of the firm, location, production facilities, legal structure and business goals. A clear description of your experience and management capabilities, as well as the expertise of other key personnel, will also be needed. If your loan applications are declined by at least two banks, you may ask the banker to make the loan under SBA's Loan Guarantee Plan or Immediate Participation Plan.

17. What kind of profits can I expect?

    Not an easy question. However, there are standards of comparison called "industry ratios" that can help you estimate your profits. Return on Investment (ROI), for example, estimates the amount of profit gained on a given number of dollars invested in the business. These ratios are broken down by Standard Industrial Classification (SIC) code and size, so you can look up your type of business to see what the industry averages are. These figures are published by several groups, and can be found at your library. Help is also available through the SBA and the trade associations that serve your industry.

18. What should I know about accounting and bookkeeping?

    The importance of keeping adequate records cannot be stressed enough. We recommend that you computerize your financial records with simple to use software programs such as Intuit's QuickBooks or other available programs. Without records, you cannot see how well your business is doing and where it is going. At a minimum, records are needed to substantiate:

    - Your tax returns under federal and state laws, including income tax and Social Security laws.
    - Your request for credit from vendors or a loan from a bank.
    - Your claims about the business, should you wish to sell it.

    But most important, you need them to run your business successfully and to increase your profits.

19. How do I set up the right record-keeping system for my business?

    The kind of records and how many you need depend on your particular operation. The SBA's resources and an accountant can provide you with many options. When deciding what is and is not necessary, keep in mind the following questions:

    - How will this record be used?
    - How important is this information likely to be?
    - Is the information available elsewhere in an equally accessible form?

20. What financial statements will I need?

    You should prepare and understand two basic financial statements:

    - The balance sheet, which is a record of assets, liabilities and capital, and
    - The income (profit-and-loss) statement, a summary of your earnings and expenses over a given period of time.

21. What does marketing involve?

    Marketing is your most important organizing tool. There are six basic aspects of marketing, called the "6 P's":

    - Product: The quality and uniqueness of item or service you sell.
    - Price: The amount you charge for your product or service.
    - Promotion: The ways you inform your market as to who, what and where you are.
    - Place: The location and distribution of your product or service.
    - Packaging: The way the business looks from the promotional materials to the dress of the staff.
    - Personnel: The level of customer service you give.

    As you can see, marketing encompasses much more than just advertising or selling. For example, a major part of marketing involves researching your customers: What do they want? What can they afford? What do they think? Your understanding and application of the answers to such questions play a major role in the success or failure of your business.

22. What is my market potential?

    The principles of determining market share and market potential are the same for all geographic areas. First determine a customer profile (who) and the geographic size of the market (how many). This is the general market potential. Knowing the number and strength of your competitors (and then estimating the share of business you will take from them) will give you the market potential specific to your enterprise.

23. What about advertising?

    Your business growth will be influenced by how well you plan and execute an advertising program. Because it is one of the main creators of your business's image, it must be well planned and well budgeted. Contact local advertising agencies or a local SBA office to assist you in devising an effective advertising strategy.

24. How do I set price levels?

    The price of a service or item is based on three basic production costs: direct materials, labor and overhead. After these costs are determined, a price is then selected that will be both profitable and competitive. Because pricing can be a complicated process, you may wish to seek help from an expert.

    Time and effort devoted to selecting where to locate your business can mean the difference between success and failure. The kind of business you are in, the potential market, availability of employees and the number of competitive establishments in your local market all determine where you should put your business.

25. Is it better to lease or buy the store (plant) and equipment?

    This is a good question and needs to be considered carefully. Leasing does not tie up your cash; a disadvantage is that the item then has no resale or salvage value since you do not own it. Careful weighing of alternatives and a cost analysis will help you make the best decision.

26. Can I operate a business from my home?

    Yes. In fact, experts estimate that as many as 20% of new small business enterprises are operated out of the owner's home. Local SBA offices and state Chambers of Commerce can provide pertinent information on how to manage a home-based business.

27. How do I find out about suppliers/manufacturers/distributors?

    Most suppliers want new accounts. A prime source for finding suppliers is the Thomas Register, which lists manufacturers by categories and geographic area. Most libraries have a directory of manufacturers listed by state. If you know the product line manufacturers, a letter or phone call to the companies will get you the local distributor-wholesaler. In some lines, trade shows are good sources of getting suppliers and looking over competing products.

28. How can the SBA help me?

    The U.S. Small Business Administration has offices in nearly every major city in the country. SBA's Office of Business Initiatives, Education and Training operates the toll-free "Answer Desk" at 1-800-368-5855, to refer callers directly to appropriate sources of information. SBA sponsors a variety of counselling, training and information services, including the Service Corps of Retired Executives (SCORE), Small Business Institutes (SBI) and Small Business Development Centers (SBDC).

29. What about telecommunications?

    All small businesses share some common functions: sales, purchasing, financing, operations and administration. Depending on your individual business, telecommunications can support your objectives in any or all of these areas. In its basic form, the telephone (the terminal) and the network (local or long distance) make up the basic components of telecommunications. It is an effective tool that can easily change with seasonality and growth. How you use telecommunications can affect how efficiently and profitably your company grows in the future.

30. What do I do when I'm ready?

    You have done your homework: You have a complete business plan; you know where you want to operate; you know how much cash you will need; and you have specific information on employee, vendor and market possibilities. You now may want someone to look over your plans objectively. Contact the business department at a local college for another opinion. A SCORE representative at the Small Business Administration can also review your work and help with the fine tuning, or get a private consultant. Then, when you have made the final decision to go ahead, it is time to call the bank and get going. Good luck!

CHAPTER FOUR

Ideas That Win!

"No army can withstand an idea whose time has come."
VICTOR HUGO

Chapter Chart

Does your business idea really have the potential to succeed? This chapter explains how to tell whether your idea will be a hit or a flop in the fickle world of business ownership. It also shows you how to turn losing ideas into winning ones.

- Opportunity is the watchword for would-be business owners. Have you found a need in the community from which you can profit?
- Market research is the magic of wizards on Madison Avenue. Learn their secrets and reap the rewards of success!
- If there isn't a need for your product or service, you may be able to create one with clever marketing techniques.
- Competition can drive the best entrepreneurs underground. Learn how to make your product or service stand out from the crowd so that customers can't help but notice.

The number one reason why you should start your own business amounts to a single word: opportunity. If you see an opportunity to provide a product or service, generate enough money to cover your expenses and fatten your bankroll, then you're definitely on your way to business success.

AN IDEA OF YOUR OWN

Where do you find opportunity? You can start by taking the time to think about your friends' and neighbors' lives. What is missing? What would make things easier, more pleasant and efficient for these people?

Some people set aside creative time—perhaps 15 minutes a day —for just such questioning, visualizing and dreaming. Indeed, many of the greatest people in history, from Moses to Mahatma Gandhi to Abraham Lincoln to Martin Luther King, Jr., have used time alone to sort things out, think things through or imagine a better way.

Others, though, feel they can't set aside 15 minutes a day out of their overbooked lives. For these people, keeping an idea notebook is a viable option. Warren Avis, of Avis Rent-a-Car fame, suggests keeping a notebook handy at all times. "You never know when a great idea will strike," he says, "and you can't trust these things to memory alone."

> As Avis, author of *Take a Chance to Be First,* put it, "Our best ideas and business missions that are based on those ideas—most often spring out of our deepest personal motivations and interests."

From time to time go through your notebook and circle the best ideas, the ones that seem to jump off the page at you, the ones you love to dream about. Nurture these ideas. They are the golden seeds of your success.

A FUNNEL TO NARROW DOWN THE NUMBER OF YOUR IDEAS

Imagine a funnel—wide at the top, narrow at the bottom. This kind of process allows you to narrow down the number of ideas you have written in your notebook. Many ideas go in at the top and only a few come out at the bottom. The way to do this is simple.

1. Enthusiasm

   First, the most important criterion for selecting your idea is personal preference. Select an idea that sparks your enthusiasm. This will help you commit your time, energy and money making your idea work. Remember, if you are not excited, who else will be? Enthusiasm for your business is essential—without it you will not succeed.

   Don't pick an idea merely because you think it is a safe investment or you've been told that it's profitable. There are no sure bets in business—and only your commitment, skills and imagination can transform your idea into reality.

2. Community

   Take a look at the opportunities in your community to see if there is a need for what you'd like to do. If you want to sell fishing equipment, for example, but few people in your area fish, it's reasonable to assume your business will not flourish. Either change ideas or locales.

3. Target Area

   Match your ideas with the needs of your target area through market research. Market research is what the wizards on Madison Avenue use to determine what consumers will buy and how much they will pay. You can use its magic, too, at little or no cost.

   You probably have enough knowledge of your neighbors to make a few educated guesses about the kinds of businesses that would attract them.

   If you live in a city, for example, you wouldn't set up a John Deere tractor dealership, would you? But you might be inclined to start a child care center, a gourmet take-out shop or a chic clothing store. The difference is that the latter businesses offer products and services that city dwellers need and use: products and services that do some of their work for them, save them time or cater to their need to look professional and stylish.

> *"Many hidden marketable needs are overlooked for years until someone spots those needs and sets out to fill them for cash. If there is a strong pent-up demand, the business explodes!"*
>
> DUANE NEWCOMB, *FORTUNE-BUILDING SECRETS OF THE RICH*

4. Do-It-Yourself Market Research

   - The SBA can help you

     Cost: FREE

     The Small Business Admistration, a government agency charged with assisting small business owners to succeed, has conducted extensive research on the problem of matching small businesses with community needs and wants.

The agency lists six basic characteristics you should know about the people you intend to rely on for a customer base. Knowing these characteristics will help you determine the kinds of products and services that appeal to the people in your market area. Knowing more about your customers will help you judge the viability of your business idea.

CHARACTERISTICS EVERY ENTREPRENEUR SHOULD KNOW ABOUT POTENTIAL CUSTOMERS

General: age, sex, family type.

Social: education level, ethnic group, religion, leisure interests.

Labor Force: type of work.

Income: sources and amounts of income.

Housing I: numbers of people per household, relationships of occupants, occupancy rate, housing in the area.

Housing II: rental versus ownership, size, housing per person.

➪ SCORE has experienced assistance

Cost: FREE

Members of SCORE, the Service Corps of Retired Executives, are an experienced group of men and women who advise small business owners free of charge. When you go to a SCORE office, you will be assigned to a counselor who has worked in an industry or business related to your inquiry. SCORE is a program of the SBA.

➪ The Census Bureau can help too!

Cost: Minimal

You can find much information about your potential market in a book published by the U.S. Chamber of Commerce and the U.S. Bureau of the Census. The Census Bureau of Population and Housing Report presents data for almost every region in the country broken down into the categories listed below.

The book has an index in the front that allows you quick, easy access to the average characteristic in each category.

CENSUS BUREAU CATEGORIES

Age by Sex

Persons per Household

Nationality

Educational Attainment

Occupation

Family (Household) Income

Number of Homes Owned

Number of Homes Rented

Number of People per Household

Value of Housing

Size of Housing

➭ The Commerce Department can help you too!

Cost: Minimal

You can also find an overview of these facts in The Urban Atlas Tract Data for SMSA, published by the U.S. Department of Commerce.

➭ Pounding the pavement

Cost: Minimal

Conduct your own research to complete the general customer profile you've constructed. One way is to drive around the neighborhood where your potential customers live. You can see for yourself the number of cars in driveways, the size and condition of the housing, the presence or absence of children's toys and overall feeling of wealth or poverty in the area.

- Test the marketplace

  Cost: FREE

  Canvass the neighborhood. Talk to people about their needs and wants and the kinds of products and services they would use. To help with your survey, a list of questions for potential customers appears on the following page.

- Consult the experts

  Cost: FREE

  Consulting experts in your community is an important component of your market research. People to contact include:

  - Teachers
  - Instructors or professors, accountants
  - Experienced business owners, business executives
  - Anyone else whose experience and knowledge leads you to believe he or she would be a useful source of advice about what the community needs and wants.

SAMPLE MARKET SURVEY QUESTIONS

1. Do people in your market currently buy products or services similar to the one you want to provide?
2. What do they like about what they're buying now? What do they dislike?
3. Can customers currently buy the product or service in their community? If not, would they like to? Have they ever been able to buy it in the community? If so, what happened?
4. At what time of the day can they buy the product or service? Is this satisfactory?
5. How many times and how often do they use the product or service? Would they use it more often if changes were made? What changes?
6. Are there any other products or services they would use if they were available in the community?

It sounds like a lot of work. It is a lot of work. But with so much money and time at stake, you need as much information and advice as possible before you start your business.

The business world, sadly, is full of people who had an idea that couldn't miss, but it did. Be armed with the right kind of information so your business story can end in success!

5. Form Specific Objectives

   CREATE A NEED!

   Good market research can take you further than identifying a community's wants and needs. It can help you create needs.

   When cellular phones first came out, did you need one? Probably not. But now that all your competitors have them you may think differently. Smart business people create needs that only they can fill.

6. Identify Your Mission and Goals

   Warren Avis of Avis Rent-a-Car believes you need to identify your mission. If you want to open a retail computer store, for example, then your mission is to sell a certain type of computer (MacIntosh? IBM clone?) for a certain type of customer (businesspeople? personal users?) in a certain kind of environment (full-service retail? budget retail? wholesale? mail order?).

Add That Extra Something

Your mission also includes supporting principles or factors that make your idea stand out from the competition. In the retail computer store, the supporting principle is this: To succeed, the store must give customers something the other stores don't.

Marty Kingman, of Computers and Such in Fort Worth, Texas, decided the "extra something" for his business would be training seminars, house calls to help customers set up their equipment, and a 24-hour telephone hotline for emergency questions. Because Kingman knew his customers' needs and wants, this simple idea enriched his business and made it a success.

7. Look at Your Competition

   Your idea doesn't have to be completely original. In fact, originality can do more harm than good because you'll have to spend time and energy educating your potential market on what your product or service is and why they need it.

   It is far easier to latch onto a familiar idea and find a way to improve it so it fills existing needs in a better and different way. By changing things a little, you can transform a good idea into an irresistible one.

   Look at your competitors. Which aspects of their product or service are being handled poorly? Which aspects are being ignored? The answers spell opportunity for you.

When analyzing and/or comparing yourself with the competition, remember the 6 P's of marketing:

1. Price
   How much do they charge? Should you charge the same, more, or less?
2. Product/Service
   What makes your product/service different from the others? What is your Unique Selling Proposition?
3. Promotion
   How does your competition promote itself? What works, what doesn't?
4. Place
   How important is location to your business? What effect does your competitors' location have on their and your business? How are their products and services distributed?
5. Packaging
   What printed material does the competition use? What is its appearance?
6. Personnel
   What customer service strategies do they use?

Know your competition and when applicable—copy success.

UPGRADING

One way to improve an idea is through upgrading. In upgrading you take a basic product and make it special by adding value or marketing it as a luxury item.

Designer blue jeans and gourmet cookies are basically the same as their more pedestrian counterparts. It's their marketing that makes them special.

DOWNGRADING

This is the opposite of upgrading. To downgrade, you strip a product of its frills and offer it at a reduced price.

Southwest Airlines eliminated all of the extras that traditionally come with an airline ticket and caught hold of a budget market in the process.

GOOD-OLD-DAYS FEATURE

Another winning competition strategy is to bring back an old idea. Wouldn't it be wonderful if doctors started making house calls again? There may be a similar good-old-days feature that you can inject into your version of an existing product or service.

BUNDLING

Bundling is another way to improve on an existing idea. Bundling means putting two or more products or services together and selling them as a package.

Stereos were once sold only by components. Then some savvy business people bundled them. They put a radio, record player, tape player and speaker in one unit. These units are still selling today to customers who don't know a woofer from a capstan.

UNBUNDLE IT

Of course, if your competition is selling bundled products, you can always unbundle them and sell each piece separately. Tout the fact that customers can put together their own grouping just the way they like it.

IS IT A GROWTH INDUSTRY?

After shaping your idea to fit your community and your competition, you need to project it into the future to see how the passage of time, social trends and the development of new technology will affect it.

Some business ideas that were money-makers a few years ago are now money-losers. Drive-in movie theaters, for example, fell victim to the gas crunch, the subcompact car and the VCR. Make sure your idea is timely.

Some business ideas flourish as new technology becomes available. The VCR spawned a new industry—video-rental clubs—because someone realized that VCRs would take off as a consumer item and would support other businesses. The home entertainment industry is considered to have strong growth potential well into the next century.

Although you shouldn't limit yourself to so-called growth industries, your chances of success will be greater if you can read the industry signs and heed them.

According to the Department of Commerce, the ten best businesses for the year 2000 and beyond will be primarily in the service industry.

TEN BEST BUSINESS BETS FOR THE 1990s AND BEYOND

- Accounting and auditing
- Beauty and personal care services
- Computer consulting
- Conference production and planning
- Child care and elder care services
- Health and fitness clubs and courses
- Housecleaning and errand services
- Real estate assistance services
- Temporary employment agencies
- Travel planning and tour organizing

THE LONGEST JOURNEY . . . THE DEVELOPMENT OF YOUR IDEA

You have an idea. It has passed through the funnel of questions and qualifications. You've examined a potential market and you've found that a specific neighborhood, community or other market is one in which your business can succeed.

Now is the time to go into action. First, you need a plan. You may need start-up capital—yours or funding from others.

The best way to begin is to write a detailed, well-thought-out business plan. Chapter Five shows you the way to write your business plan.

Get ready to map your road to success!

CHAPTER FIVE

The Business Plan

"A business without a plan is like a ship without a rudder. Whichever way the wind blows is the way you'll go."

Chapter Chart

A business plan is a necessary tool for developing almost any business idea. This chapter explains how to write a business plan that will yield results for you.

- The major components of the business plan are the business description, the marketing plan and the financial plan. Each takes up a specific aspect of your business life.
- It's important to work on your goals until they are clear. Fuzzy goals make it difficult to tell whether you and your employees have met them.
- You don't have to be a genius to work up the financial section of your plan. A few brief tables are all you need to show the financial picture of your idea.

You have your idea. You have done a lot of thinking about what you can do for your business and what it can do for you. You also have a fair understanding of who your business will serve and how you will make your product or service appealing.

Your next task is to focus on how you are going to make your business idea into a successful venture.

TAKE TIME TO SAVE TIME

Most budding entrepreneurs like to skip a detailed planning phase. But, like it or not, it is an essential part of most successful businesses.

Business plans are important documents that organize all of the brainstorming you did in previous chapters into a comprehensive plan. It tells the story about what you plan to do and how you plan to do it. It can make a statement about you and your managerial abilities. It can help to convince a lender that you have what it takes to succeed.

Writing a business plan has many benefits:

- It helps you focus on your idea, collect your thoughts and organize them in a logical, winning manner.
- It is a persuasive tool in convincing your family, friends, associates and potential funding agents that you are committed to being an entrepreneur with a winning idea.
- It proves that you are not only innovative, but also realistic.
- It gives the particulars of how you will use the money passing through your checking account each month. This information is invaluable to you and your banker because a business that does not control its cash flow is a short-lived one.
- It serves as a road map through the development of your business and will help you focus on achieving success.

Many entrepreneurs think they do not have to plan because they knew their businesses. Don't let such self-important talk fool you.

For most people, however, the business plan is a practical storehouse of our most brilliant business ideas. It is our road map to success.

Even though it takes more time for you to draw up your business plan, doing so will save you time, money and trouble in the long run. If you know where you are going, you will not have to hesitate on your options when three contractors are on the line and a dozen impatient customers are at your door.

ANATOMY OF A BUSINESS PLAN

The Business Plan—What It Includes

What goes into a business plan? This is an excellent question to ask—and one that many new and potential small business owners should ask, but often do not. The body of the business plan can be divided into four distinctive sections:

1. Description of the business
2. Marketing plan
3. Management plan
4. Financial management plan

Addenda to the business plan should include the executive summary, supporting documents and financial projections.

Description of the Business

In this section, a detailed description of your business is presented. An excellent question to ask yourself is "What business am I in?" In answering this question include your products, market and services as well as a thorough description of what makes your business unique. Remember, however, that as you develop your business plan, you may have to modify or revise your initial questions.

The business description is divided into three primary sections—a description of the business, a description of the product or service you will be offering, and a description of the location of your business, and why this location is desirable.

1. BUSINESS DESCRIPTION

When describing your business, generally you should explain:

1. Legalities—business form: proprietorship, partnership, corporation, business. What licenses or permits you will need.
2. Business type: merchandising, manufacturing or service.
3. What your product or service is.
4. If it is a new independent business, a takeover, or an expansion.

5. Why your business will be profitable. What are the growth opportunities? How will franchising affect growth opportunities?
6. When your business will be open (days, hours). Are certain operating hours required by the landlord or business company?
7. What you have learned about your kind of business from outside sources (trade suppliers, bankers, other business owners, publications).

A cover sheet goes before the description. It includes the name, address and telephone number of the business, and the names of all principals. In the description of your business, describe its unique aspects and how or why they will appeal to consumers. Emphasize any special features that you feel will appeal to customers and explain how and why these features are appealing.

The description of your business should clearly identify goals and objectives, and it should clarify why you are, or why you want to be in business.

2. PRODUCT/SERVICE

Try to describe the benefits of your goods and services from your customers' perspective. Successful business owners know or at least have an idea of what their customers want or expect from them. This type of anticipation can be helpful in building customer satisfaction and loyalty. And it certainly is a good strategy for beating the competition or retaining your competitiveness. Describe:

1. What you are selling.
2. How your product or service will benefit the customer.
3. Which products/services (in your case, the business) are in demand; if there will be a steady flow of cash.
4. What is different about the product or service your business is offering.

3. THE LOCATION

The location of your business can play a decisive role in its success or failure. Your location should be built around your customers, it should be accessible and it should provide a sense of security.

Consider these questions when addressing this section of your business plan:

1. What are your location's needs?
2. What kind of space will you need?
3. Why is the area desirable? Why is a particular building desirable?
4. Is it easily accessible? Is public transportation available? Is street lighting adequate?
5. Are market shifts or demographic shifts occurring?

It may be a good idea to make a checklist of questions you identify when developing your business plan. Categorize your questions, and as you answer each one, remove it from your list.

The Marketing Plan

Marketing plays a vital role in successful business ventures. How well you market your business, along with a few other considerations, will ultimately determine your degree of success or failure. The key element of a successful marketing plan is to know your customers—their likes, dislikes, expectations. By identifying these factors, you can develop a marketing strategy that will allow you to arouse and fulfill their needs.

Identify your customers by their age, sex, income/educational level and residence. At first, target only those customers who are most likely to purchase your product or service. As your customer base expands, then, you may need to consider modifying the marketing plan to include other customers.

Develop a marketing plan for your business by answering these questions:

1. Who are your customers? Define your target market(s).
2. Are your markets growing? steady? declining?
3. Is your business market share growing? steady? declining?
4. Are your markets large enough to expand?
5. How will you attract, hold, increase your market share? How will you promote your sales?
6. What is the pricing strategy?

Chapter Six contains a sample Marketing Plan and Marketing Tips, Tricks & Traps, a condensed guide on how to market your product or service. Study these documents carefully when developing the marketing portion of your business plan.

1. COMPETITION

Competition is a way of life. We compete for jobs, promotions, scholarships to institutes of higher learning, we compete in sports—and in almost every aspect of our lives. Nations compete for the consumer in the global marketplace as do individual business owners. Advances in technology can send the profit margins of a successful business into a tailspin causing them to plummet overnight or within a few hours. When considering these and other factors, we can conclude that business is a highly competitive, volatile arena. Because of this, it is important to know your competitors.

Questions like these can help you.

1. Who are your five nearest direct competitors?
2. Who are your indirect competitors?
3. How are their businesses: steady? increasing? decreasing?
4. What have you learned from their operations? from their advertising?
5. What are their strengths? weaknesses?
6. How does their product or service differ from yours?

Start a file on each of your competitors. Keep manila envelopes of their advertising and promotional materials and their pricing strategy techniques. Review these files periodically, determining when and how often they advertise, sponsor promotions and offer sales. Study the copy used in the advertising and promotional materials, and their sales strategy. For example, is their copy short, descriptive, catchy? How much do they reduce prices for sales? Using this technique can help you to better understand your competitors and how they operate their businesses.

2. PRICING AND SALES

Your pricing strategy is another marketing technique you can use to improve your overall competitiveness. It may be a good idea to get a feel for the pricing strategy your competitors are using. That way you can determine if your prices are in line with competitors in your market area, and if they are in line with industry averages.

Some of the pricing strategies that you may consider, depending on the type of business, are:

- retail cost and pricing
- competitive position
- pricing below competition
- pricing above competition
- price lining
- multiple pricing
- service costs and pricing (for service businesses only)
- service components
- material costs
- labor costs
- overhead costs

The key to success is to have a well-planned strategy, to establish your policies and to constantly monitor prices and operating costs to ensure profits. It is a good policy to keep abreast of the changes in the marketplace because these changes can affect your competitiveness and profit margins.

3. ADVERTISING AND PUBLIC RELATIONS

How you advertise and promote your business may make or break your business. Having a good product or service and not advertising and promoting it is like not having a business at all. Many business owners operate under the mistaken concept that the business will promote itself, and channel money that should be used for advertising and promotions to other areas of the business. Advertising and promotions, however, are the lifeline of a business and should be treated as such.

Devise a plan that uses advertising and networking as a means to promote your business. Develop short, descriptive copy (text material) that clearly identifies your goods or services, location and price. Use catchy phrases to arouse the interest of your readers, listeners or viewers. Make sure the advertisements you create are consistent with the image you are trying to project. Remember the more care and attention you devote to your marketing program, the more successful your business will be.

The Management Plan

Managing your business requires more than just the desire to be your own boss. It demands dedication, persistence, the ability to make decisions and the ability to manage both employees and finances. Your management plan, along with your marketing and financial management plans, sets the foundation for and facilitates the success of your business.

Like plants and equipment, people are resources—they are the most valuable asset a business has. You will soon discover that employees and staff will play an important role in the total operation of your business. Consequently, it's imperative that you know what skills you possess and those you lack, since you will have to hire personnel to supply the skills you don't have. Additionally, it is imperative that you know how to manage and treat your employees. Make them a part of the team. Keep them informed of and get their feedback regarding changes. Employees often have excellent ideas that can lead to new market areas, innovations to existing products or services or new product lines or services that can improve your overall competitiveness.

Your management plan should answer questions such as:

- How does your background/business experience help you in this business?
- What are your weaknesses, and how can you compensate for them?
- Who will be on the management team?
- What are their strengths/weaknesses?
- What are their duties?
- Are these duties clearly defined?
- Will this assistance be ongoing?
- What are your current personnel needs?
- What are your plans for hiring and training personnel?
- Who will provide training for you and the management team?
- What salaries, benefits, vacations, holidays will you offer?
- What benefits, if any, can you afford at this point?

The operating procedures, manuals and materials should be included in this section of the business plan. Study these documents carefully when writing your business plan, and be sure to incorporate this material. Develop a management plan that will ensure the success of your business and satisfy the needs and expectations of employees.

The Financial Management Plan

Sound financial management is one of the best ways for your business to remain profitable and solvent. How well you manage the finances of your business is the cornerstone of every successful business venture. Each year thousands of potentially successful businesses fail because of poor financial management. As a business owner, you will need to identify and implement policies that will ensure that you meet your financial objectives.

To effectively manage your finances, plan a sound, realistic budget by determining the actual amount of money needed to open your business (start-up costs) and the amount needed to keep it open (operating costs). The first step to building a sound financial plan is to devise a start-up budget. Your start-up budget will usually include such one-time-only costs as major equipment, utility deposits, down payments, etc.

The start-up budget should allow for these expenses:

- personnel (costs prior to opening)
- occupancy
- licenses/permits
- equipment
- insurance
- advertising/promotions
- supplies
- salaries/wages
- accounting
- legal/professional fees
- income
- utilities
- payroll expenses

An operating budget is prepared when you are actually ready to open for business. The operating budget will reflect your priorities in terms of how you spend your money, the expenses you will incur and how you will meet those expenses (income). Your operating budget also should include money to cover the first three to six months of operation.

The operating budget should allow for the following expenses:

- personnel
- rent
- loan payments
- legal/accounting
- supplies
- salaries/wages
- dues/subscriptions/fees
- repairs/maintenance
- insurance
- depreciation
- advertising/promotions
- payroll expenses
- utilities
- taxes
- miscellaneous expenses

The financial section of your business plan should include any loan applications you've filed, a capital equipment and supply list, balance sheet, breakeven analysis, pro-forma income projections (profit- and loss-statement) and pro-forma cash flow. The income statement and cash flow projections should include a three-year summary, detail by month for the first year, and detail by quarter for the second and third years.

The accounting system and the inventory control system that you will be using is generally addressed in this section of the business plan also. Whether you develop the accounting and inventory systems yourself or have an outside financial advisor develop them, you will need to acquire a thorough understanding of each and how it operates. Your financial advisor can assist you in developing this section of your business plan.

The following questions should help you determine the amount of start-up capital you will need to purchase and open your business.

- What is your capital reserve?
- How much money will you need to purchase your business?
- Will you need additional capital for start-up?
- How much cash will be needed for working capital?

Other questions that you will need to consider are:

- What type of accounting system will you use? Is it a single-entry or double-entry system?
- What are your sales goals and profit goals for the coming year?

- What financial projections will you need to include in your business plan?
- What kind of inventory control system will you use?

Your plan should include an explanation of all projections. Unless you are thoroughly familiar with financial statements, get help in preparing your cash flow and income statements and your balance sheet. Your aim is not to become a financial wizard, but to understand the financial tools well enough to gain their benefits. Your accountant or financial advisor can help you accomplish this goal.

A more thorough discussion of the financial section of your business plan is presented in the next chapter.

On the following pages are two forms we've used to establish goals, develop plans, and achieve results.

Goal Worksheet

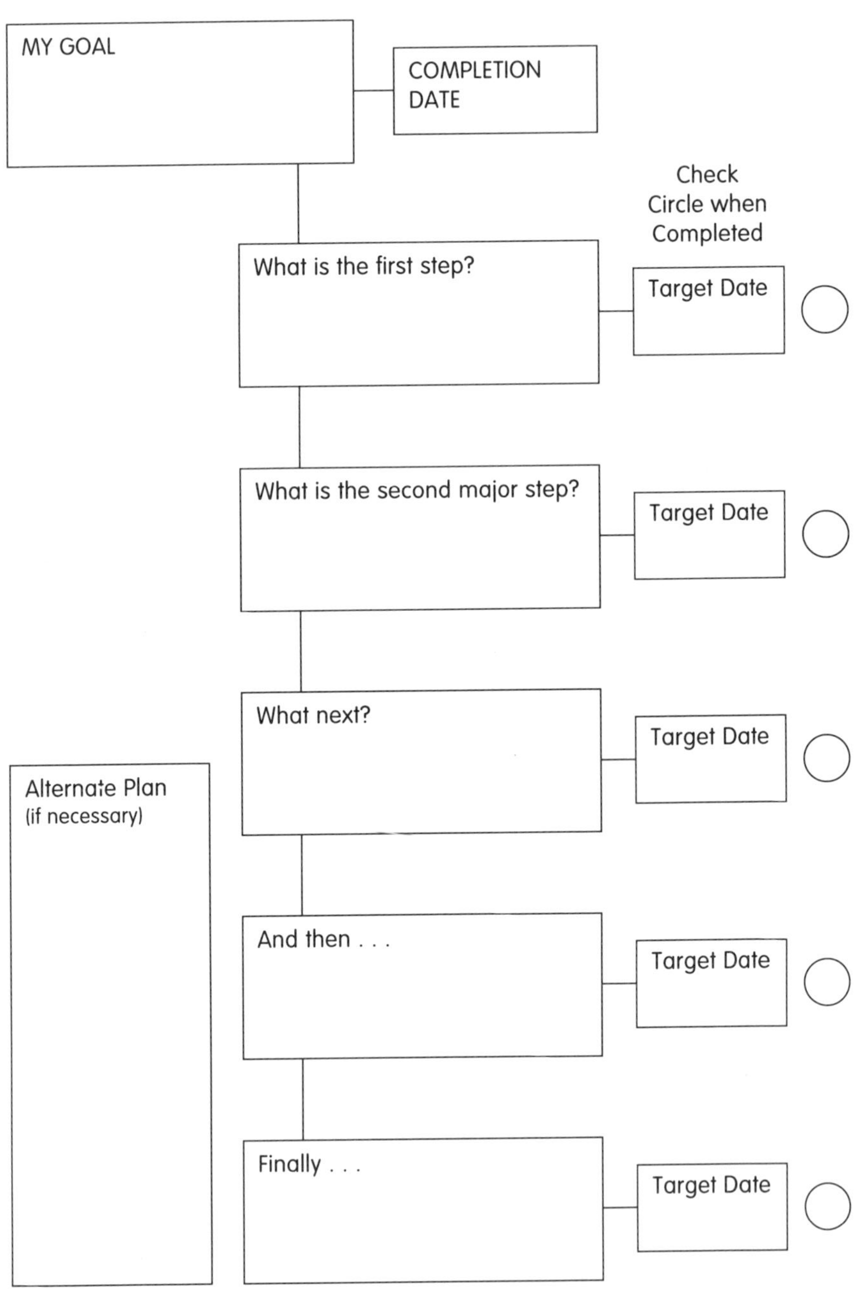

Planning Worksheet . . . Roadmap

GOAL:

Action Step	Specific Steps and Resource Requirements (people, money, material, space)	Coordination Requirements	Target Dates		Evaluation
			Begin	End	

CHAPTER SIX

The Marketing Plan

Chapter Chart

How will you market your products and services? What is your competitive strategy? Will you compete on price, quality or service? This chapter will show you what you need to know and look for in order to make these crucial decisions.

- ➩ You must do thorough marketing research to determine your place in the marketplace. Marketing research is especially important when large amounts of capital are at risk.
- ➩ One of the keys to your success will be in designing a benefit-based advertising and promotions program. These two important components of your marketing effort should communicate to your customers how you are different from your competitors, why people should do business with you, and many other important factors.
- ➩ Your pricing strategy must be determined so that customers perceive and realize benefits or values at whatever price you decide upon. Higher prices should result in higher profit margins. But the price really depends on what it costs you to add the additional value. Care must be taken to ensure that your enterprise is profitable.

Marketing Plan: Marketing Your Business For Success

Understanding the Marketplace

Marketing plays a vital role in successful business ventures. How well you develop your marketing plan, along with your management and financial management plans, will ultimately determine your degree of success or failure. The key elements of a successful marketing plan are to 1) know your customers—their likes, dislikes and expectations, 2) know your competitors—their strengths and weaknesses and 3) know your product or service. By identifying these factors, you can develop a marketing strategy that will allow you to arouse and fulfill customers needs, better understand competitors and identify changes in the marketplace that can affect your bottom line.

The purpose of the marketing plan is to define your market, i.e., identify your customers and competitors, outline a strategy for attracting and keeping customers, and identify and anticipate change. Your business will not succeed simply because you want it to succeed. It takes careful planning and a thorough understanding of the marketplace to develop a strategy that will ensure success.

Generally, the first and most important step in understanding the market is to study it through market research. Determine what product or service you plan to offer and write a description of it. Knowing your product or service is a key variable in a successful marketing plan. Writing a description of your product or service is the first step and, perhaps, one of the most important steps in developing an effective marketing program. It is during this initial phase that you will begin to get to know your product or service intimately. When describing your product or service, outline what you feel are its unique aspects, and explain how or why these aspects will appeal to customers. Emphasize the special features that you feel are its selling points. These features are what you will use to persuade customers to purchase your product or service.

Next begin developing your sales projections by determining if there is a demand for your product or service. Study the data that you have collected. This will help you understand how the marketplace operates relative to your product/service, and it can help you develop the skills to identify and anticipate changes in the marketplace. Start your own file on marketplace trends. Periodically review your data, comparing it with current trends and looking for shifts in the market. If changes are occurring, you need to be aware of them and you should modify your marketing plan to coincide with them. Wise business owners periodically update their marketing plans to reflect changes in the marketplace and to keep their marketing programs current.

A marketing plan should answer these questions:

- Is this product or service in constant demand?
- How many competitors provide the same product or service?
- Can you create a demand for your product or service?
- Can you effectively compete in price, quality and delivery?
- Will the price of the product or service give you the projected profit you've outlined?

Review the marketing data that you have collected to make sure it answers these questions. If it doesn't, you will need to gather additional data that will offer viable answers to these questions. When you are satisfied that you have a fairly good understanding of how the market operates and how to identify market shifts and trends, start writing the marketing section of your business plan.

To a large extent, the success of your business depends on how well you promote it. Many small business owners think that by simply running an advertisement or a classified ad in the local newspaper, the business will market itself. How wrong they are! It is your responsibility to promote your product or service by cultivating the marketplace, i.e., attracting and keeping customers. You can accomplish this goal by knowing your market, your customers, your competitors and your product/service. Periodically review and reassess the data you gathered during the market research process and compare it with current market data. By doing so, you will be better able to determine if your program is in line with your competitors, if it is in line with industry averages, and what adjustments you can make to improve your overall competitiveness.

A sample marketing plan is attached as part of this chapter. Study it carefully, then try to develop a similar program for your business.

MARKET RESEARCH

Strategies for Researching the Market

Researching your market is perhaps the easiest way to assess it. Market research does not have to be costly, nor does it have to be a complex process. It can be as simple and as easy as surveying a cross-section of your consumers (focus group) to get their opinions about the product or service you will be offering, or conducting a telephone or mail survey. The disadvantage of using the telephone or mail survey method is the individuals you contact may not be interested in responding to a survey. Other market research techniques include analyzing demographic data, such as population growth/decline rates, age range, sex, income and educational levels; brainstorming with family and friends; and conducting focus group interviews. Whatever method you use, your focus should be on gathering enough information to determine who your potential customers will be—their needs, wants and expectations; if there is a demand for your product or service; who your competitors are and how well they are doing.

Market research should answer questions such as:

- Who are your customers and potential customers?
- What are their buying habits?
- Where do they live?
- Can and will they buy the product or service you're offering?
- Are you offering the kinds of goods or services they want—at the best place, the best time and in the best amounts?
- Are your prices consistent with what the buyers view as the products' value?
- Are your promotional programs working?
- Are you applying the promotional programs in a way that will bring about success?
- What do customers think of your business?
- Who are your competitors?
- How does your business compare with the competition?

While there are some disadvantages to market research—it can be a costly, time-consuming process—the advantages outweigh the disadvantages. Don't forgo this process or stop halfway because you are not getting the desired results. This may be an indication that you are going into the wrong business or that there isn't a market for your product or service. Don't be discouraged. You may simply need to modify your original plan, or you may need to select a different kind of business.

A few of the benefits of market research are these:

- Learning who your customers are and what they want.
- Learning how to reach your customers and how frequently you should try to communicate with them.
- Learning which appeals are most effective and which ones aren't.
- Learning the relative successes of different marketing strategies in relation to their return on investment.

While market research is a tedious, time-consuming process, it is necessary if you want to be successful. Think of market research as simply a method of finding out what catches customers' attention, and as an organized way of finding objective answers to critical business questions. Market research focuses and organizes marketing information, ensuring that it is timely and that it provides what you need to:

- Reduce business risks.
- Spot problems and potential problems in your current market.
- Identify and profit from sales opportunities.
- Get basic facts about your markets to help you make better decisions and set up plans of action.

If viewed from this standpoint, market research is an invaluable tool that can save you time, effort and money.

WHAT DOES A MARKETING PLAN CONTAIN?

Many first-time business owners think that by simply placing an ad in a local newspaper or a commercial on a radio or a television station, customers will automatically flock to purchase their product or service. This is true to a certain extent. Some people are likely to learn about your product or service and try it, just out of curiosity. But hundreds, even thousands of other potential customers may never learn of your business. Just think of the money you'll lose, simply because you didn't develop an adequate marketing program!

Marketing is an essential part of business operations. And it often determines how successful your business will be. What you as a potential small business owner must do is acquire a thorough understanding of the marketing process and use it to extract advantages from the marketplace. Go over the strategies and techniques you have developed until you understand how to apply them to get the results you desire. Remember, your aim is not only to attract and keep a steady group of loyal customers, but also to expand your customer base by identifying and attracting new customers and reduce risks by anticipating market shifts that can affect your bottom line.

To help you accomplish this aim, your marketing plan should include strategies typical of any marketing plan. The plan should especially include what marketeers dub the 6 P's of marketing (price, product/service, promotion, place, packaging, and personnel).

You should develop a marketing plan using the strategies listed below. Include a brief explanation for each strategy.

- Describe the target market by
  - age
  - sex
  - profession/career
  - income level
  - educational level
  - residence

  Know your customers better than you know anyone—their likes, dislikes, expectations. Since you will have limited resources, target only those customers who are more likely to purchase your product or service. As your business grows and your customer base expands, then you may need to consider modifying this section of the marketing plan to include other customers.

- Identify competition
  - market research data
  - demand for product or service
  - nearest direct and indirect competitors
  - strengths and weaknesses of competitors
  - assessment of how competitors' businesses are doing
  - description of the unique features of your product or service

- similarities and dissimilarities between your product or service and competitors'
- pricing strategy for and comparison of yours with the competition's

Identify the five nearest direct and indirect competitors. Start a file on each identifying their weaknesses and strengths. Keep files on their advertising and promotional materials and their pricing strategies. Review these files periodically to determine when and how often they advertise, sponsor promotions and offer sales.

➪ Describe product/service

Try to describe the benefits of your good(s) or service(s) from your customers' perspective. Emphasize special features—i.e., the selling points. Successful business owners know or at least have an idea of what their customers want or expect from them. Your product or service should be a reflection of these expectations. This type of anticipation can be helpful in building customer satisfaction and loyalty.

➪ Develop marketing budget

- advertising and promotional plan
- costs allocated for advertising and promotions
- advertising and promotional materials
- list of advertising media to be used

Operating an effective marketing plan requires money, so you will have to allocate funds from your operating budget to cover advertising, promotional and all other costs associated with marketing. Develop a marketing budget based on the cost of the media you will use, and the cost for collecting research data and monitoring shifts in the marketplace.

➪ Describe location (place)

- description of the location
- advantages and disadvantages of location

Again, try to describe the location of your business from your customers' perspective. Describe its assets—i.e., the convenience, whether public transportation is accessible, safety aspects (street lighting, well-lit parking lot or facility), decor, etc. Your location should be built around your customers, it should be accessible and it should provide a sense of security.

➩ Develop pricing strategy
- pricing techniques with brief descriptions
- retail costing and pricing
- competitive position
- pricing below competition
- pricing above competition
- pricing according to product/service lines
- multiple pricing
- service costs and pricing (for service businesses only)
- service components
- material costs
- labor costs
- overhead costs

Study your pricing strategy and the strategies used by competitors. That way you will acquire a thorough understanding of how to price your product or service, and you can determine if your prices are in line with competitors, if they are in line with industry averages and what adjustments you can make to bring them in line.

The key to success is to have a well-planned strategy, to establish your policies, and to constantly monitor prices and operating costs to ensure profits. Keep abreast of changes in the marketplace because these changes can affect your bottom line.

➩ Develop an effective promotional strategy
- advertising media
- print media (newspaper, magazine, classified ads, yellow pages advertising, brochure)
- radio
- television
- networking

- business cards
- tee shirts, hats, buttons, pens

Develop a promotional strategy that uses various media for promoting your business. Monitor the different media, identifying those that most effectively promote your business. Concentrate on developing material for these formats that clearly identify your goods or services, location and price. Since financial institutions weigh the soundness of your marketing plan when deciding whether your business is a good risk for their money, it is important that you prepare and present credible market data that shows there is a need in the community for your business and that demonstrates your ability to compete successfully.

THE MARKETING PLAN: ITS ADVANTAGES AND DISADVANTAGES

A well-written, comprehensive marketing plan is the focal point of all business ventures because it describes how you plan to attract and retain customers—the most crucial aspect of a business. And why are customers so important? The answer is simple. They ultimately are the means by which you will generate the income needed for daily operations, repaying debts and turning a profit. In essence the customers are your lifeline and the marketing plan is the pipeline that allows you access to them.

The marketing plan is essential to any successful business, and your business is no exception. It is the heart of the business, the basis from which all other operational and management plans are derived. Marketing offers you a wealth of information that, if applied correctly, can virtually ensure the success of your business. Therefore, it is important that you, as a first-time business owner, develop a comprehensive, effective marketing program. If you need assistance in accomplishing this task, contact your local SBA office. (Consult the local telephone directory under U.S. Government for the telephone number and address of the SBA office nearest you.)

Advantages/Disadvantages of Developing a Marketing Plan

An effective marketing plan will certainly boost your sales and increase your profit margins, which should be the goal of every business owner. It is a milepost down the road to success, and as such, care and time should be put into its development. You must be able to convince customers that you have the best product or service for them at the best possible price. If you cannot do so, then you are wasting your time and money. This is where the marketing plan comes into play, and this is why it is so important.

There are numerous advantages you can extract from the marketplace if you know how. The marketing plan is an excellent tool for identifying and developing strategies for extracting these advantages.

A few of the advantages are outlined below. Study these strategies, then include them in your marketing plan.

- Identifies needs and wants of consumers
- Determines demand for product or service
- Aids in design of products/services that fulfill consumer needs
- Outlines measures for generating the cash for daily operations, repaying debts and turning a profit
- Identifies competitors and analyzes your firm's competitive advantage
- Identifies new product/service areas
- Identifies new and/or potential customers
- Allows for test to see if strategies are giving the desired results

Some of the potential disadvantages of the marketing plan are:

- Leads to faulty marketing decisions based on improperly analyzed data
- Creates unrealistic financial projections if information is interpreted incorrectly

Remember, the advantages of the marketing plan outweigh the drawbacks, so seek professional assistance when developing the marketing section of your business plan. It will be worth the investment.

OUTLINE FOR A MARKETING PLAN

Elements of a Marketing Plan

I. Description of the Target Market
- age
- sex
- profession
- income level
- educational level
- residence

II. Description of Competitors
- market research data
- demand for product or service
- nearest direct and indirect competitors
- strengths and weaknesses of competitors
- assessment of how competitors' businesses are doing
- description of the unique features of your product or service
- similarities and dissimilarities between your product or service and competitors

III. Description of Product/Service
- describe your product or service
- emphasize special features, i.e., the selling points

IV. Marketing Budget
- advertising and promotional plan
- costs allocated for advertising and promotions
- advertising and promotional materials
- list of advertising media to be used and estimate of cost for each medium

V. Description of Location (Place)
- description of the location
- advantages and disadvantages of location

VI. Pricing Strategy
- pricing techniques and brief description of these techniques
- retail costing and pricing (for retail businesses only)
- competitive position
- pricing below competition
- pricing above the competition
- price lining
- multiple pricing (for service businesses only)
- service components
- material costs
- labor costs
- overhead costs

DEVELOPING AN EFFECTIVE MARKETING STRATEGY

A few of the advantages of developing the marketing plan for your business are that you get first-hand experience in conducting market research and in actually writing the marketing plan, and you get to know your business intimately—a trademark of all successful business owners. Developing the marketing plan, like all other aspects of the business plan, is a very time consuming process, but one you need to undergo to operate a successful enterprise.

No matter how well-written and comprehensive your marketing plan may be, this aspect alone doesn't ensure that you will attract customers to your business or even maintain a stream of steady, loyal customers. How well your advertisements and promotions draw customers will ultimately determine how effective your marketing strategy is.

When selecting your market and location, try to select an area where the market isn't over saturated with businesses offering products or services similar to yours, or try to select an area where the market isn't declining. Whatever location you select, it is your responsibility to cultivate your market. One of the easiest ways to do this is through advertising and promotions. Remember the aim of the advertising and promotional strategy is to create awareness of your product or service, arouse customers' needs and expectations to the point of consumption and create a loyal stream of satisfied customers who continue to patronize your business.

EFFECTIVE ADVERTISING AND PROMOTIONAL TECHNIQUES

Perhaps, the first step in developing an effective advertising and promotional strategy is to understand the difference between the two concepts. Most people think that advertising and promotions are one and the same; there is, however, a distinct difference between the two. While both advertising and promotions use the different media formats—print, radio and television—as a way of conveying a message, promotion encompasses much more. It is a method of advertising that can entail community involvement. This could mean sponsoring a Boy or Girl Scout troop, allowing non-profit organizations to use your facility (e.g., letting the high school drama club use your parking lot for a car wash fund raiser), sending an underprivileged child to day camp or becoming involved in any type of positive community activity that will bring attention to your business.

While advertising is a way of keeping your business in the public's eye, promotions can be a way of signaling your commitment to your business as well as your concern about and commitment to the community and its residents. This commitment may be one of the most effective techniques you can develop for building customer loyalty. People tend to be more supportive of businesses and organizations that give something back to the community, rather than those that simply take from the community, never giving anything in return.

Now, let's look at how to develop effective advertising and promotional programs for your business.

THE KEY TO A SUCCESSFUL ADVERTISING AND PROMOTIONAL PLAN

Advertising

Advertising plays an important role in successful business ventures. It entails identifying and selecting the media that provide the greatest amount of exposure for your business and developing effective, yet appropriate materials for each medium. It is more than running an ad in a local newspaper, on a radio or television station or just simply hanging a sign outside your business and waiting for customers to purchase your product or service. It requires that you know your product or service—that is, the selling points—and that you develop literature that can arouse the customers' consciousness to the point that they are curious enough to investigate it, and then raise their need or desire to the point that they are willing to purchase it.

Advertising keeps your product or service in the public's eye by creating a sense of awareness. Yet this awareness alone will not ensure the success of your business. Thus, advertising not only has to be effective, it must also be continuous.

When developing an effective advertising strategy for your business, it may be a good idea to review the advertising materials of competitors and other businesses offering the same or similar products or services. Develop materials that can be applied regionally and locally and select the media that will provide the greatest amount of exposure and the most effective means of promoting your business.

Since advertising can be costly, try to use a medium that is cost effective, yet will effectively market your business. If this is not possible, then be prepared to spend whatever is necessary to advertise your business effectively—the outcome will be worth the investment.

It may be a good idea to mix the different media formats that you use. For example, design a brochure that describes your product or service, emphasizing its selling points (special features). Place copies of the brochure in strategic locations to use as customer handouts. Or, devise a customer survey. The survey should focus on whether customers like the product or service, the quality of the product/service, ways to improve it, and the quality of service provided by staff—their friendliness and courtesy. Place the survey with a self-addressed, stamped envelope near the check-out counter and ask customers to mail it back or bring it when they return. Review their comments with your staff and implement those suggestions that are practical and cost efficient and can improve the overall quality of service your business provides.

Other media formats to use are:

- Newspaper, radio or television ads (newspaper advertising is the least expensive and television advertising is the most expensive of these formats). You probably will need professional advice and assistance when developing ads for these media
- Business cards
- Classified ads in the local newspaper
- Direct marketing
- Telemarketing (this format can be expensive also)
- Yellow Pages advertising
- Sampling—mailing or distributing free samples of your product to the public or posting a flyer about your service in public areas
- Advertising in community-based magazines, newspapers or trade association magazines

- Networking (perhaps the most effective and least expensive technique)

Whatever media format you use, be willing to invest the money needed to develop an effective ad campaign.

Promotions

As discussed earlier, promotion entails more than just selecting the media format to market your business. It can and often does encompass community involvement. This involvement can range from sponsoring a Boy or Girl Scout troop to hosting a charity ball for senior citizens or allowing non-profit organizations to use your facility.

Your approach to promotion should encompass more than creating a sense of awareness about your business. It should include a commitment to community involvement—the desire to give something back to the community and its residents. An excellent way to foster this type of involvement is to meet with community leaders to find out how you can help, and what events are forthcoming that could require your assistance. Keep in mind that community leaders can be an excellent networking tool for getting the word out about your business, especially if they feel your involvement is genuine. Community leaders are very influential and this connection can prove to be a good, inexpensive way to network.

These are examples of some ways you can participate in community programs:

- Sponsor a Boy or Girl Scout troop for summer camp.
- Sponsor an underprivileged child in day camp.
- Host and sponsor a charity ball for senior citizens.
- Sponsor cooperative education for high school and/or college students.
- Volunteer as a tutor for at-risk students (those likely to drop out or fail in school).
- Sponsor a fund raiser for the homeless or provide day-care tuition assistance for children of single-parent households.
- Offer summer employment to local high school, middle school and college students.

- Become active in the local chapters of the Big Brothers or Big Sisters organizations.
- Volunteer in a local literacy program.

Other inexpensive ways of promoting your business that don't entail community involvement are:

- Employee tee shirts, hats, aprons or jackets with the name of your business, and ball point pens with the name, telephone number and logo of your business
- Balloons with the name, telephone number and logo of your business
- Free samples
- A door prize for the 100th or 1000th customer to enter your business

While it is impossible for you to participate in every event or program in the community, you should consider at least getting involved in one or two activities, even if it's only on a part-time basis. People tend to be more supportive of businesses, organizations or individuals that give something to the community. And this is the image you especially want to project in your promotional activities.

No plan that you or anyone develops will show you how to promote or advertise your business. These are techniques that you yourself will have to develop. Talk it over with your family and community leaders, then decide which activities you can afford to sponsor and have the time to commit to before becoming involved. Involvement in the community doesn't necessarily have a price tag attached. Find a project that you can afford (if money is required), for which you have time and which is of interest to you.

Still other cost effective ways to promote your business include:

- Direct mail solicitations—sending literature or free samples to residents, briefly explaining the product or service you are offering, the location of your business, and operating hours. A direct mail solicitation can include both literature and free samples depending on the type of business that you are operating.

- Grand openings and special events—making prospective customers aware of your business and the product or service you are offering by inviting them to an open house celebration. During the celebration you can serve refreshments, give a tour of the facility, or give prizes or gifts to guests.
- Developing leads—this method entails identifying who is in the market for your product or service and making them aware of what you have to offer.
- Promoting image and goodwill—reliability, quality products, fair prices, fast service and concern for customers are typical images businesses like to portray.
- Introducing new products and services—when you are offering prospects something they haven't seen before from you or perhaps from anyone else, you have to tell them about it. Develop advertising materials that describe the new service or product you are offering and identify its unique qualities (the selling points).

There is no single formula to show you how to effectively advertise or promote your business. These are skills you develop with time. You may have to try a lot of different techniques before you discover one or more that most effectively market your business. What you will need to do is try different techniques over a period of time, evaluate the results and then select the techniques that are cost efficient and get the word out about your business.

For ideas on how to develop an effective advertising and promotional strategy, see Marketing Tips, Tricks & Traps, further along in this chapter. A sample marketing plan also is included to assist you in developing an effective marketing strategy for your business. The table, Advertising/Promotional Strategic Mix, will help you outline a strategy for advertising and promoting your business, while monitoring costs.

THE ENTREPRENEUR'S MARKETING PLAN

This is the marketing plan of ______________________________

I. MARKET ANALYSIS

A. Target Market—Who are the customers?

1. We will be selling primarily to (check all that apply):

		Total Percent of Business
a. Private Sector	________	________
b. Wholesalers	________	________
c. Retailers	________	________
d. Government	________	________
e. Other	________	________

2. We will be targeting customers by:

a. Product Line/Services
We will target specific lines ________

b. Geographic Area? Which Areas? ________

c. Sales? We will target sales of ________

d. Industry? Our target industry is ________

e. Other? ________

3. How much will our selected market spend on our type of product or service this coming year? $________

B. Competition

1. Who are our competitors?

NAME ______________________________

ADDRESS ______________________________

____

Years in Business ________

Market Share ________

Price/Strategy ________

Product/Service Features ________

NAME ______________________________

ADDRESS ______________________________

____

Years in Business ____________

Market Share ____________

Price/Strategy ____________

Product/Service Features ____________

2. How competitive is the market?

   High ____________

   Medium ____________

   Low ____________

3. List below our strengths and weaknesses compared to our competition (consider such areas as location, size of resources, reputation, services, personnel, etc.):

Strengths	Weaknesses
1. ____________	1. ____________
2. ____________	2. ____________
3. ____________	3. ____________
4. ____________	4. ____________

C. Environment

1. The following are some important economic factors that will affect our product or service (such as country growth, industry health, economic trends, taxes, rising energy prices, etc.):

   ____

   ____

   ____

2. The following are some important legal factors that will affect our market:

   ____

   ____

   ____

3. The following are some important government factors:

4. The following are other environmental factors that will affect our market, but over which we have no control:

II. PRODUCT OR SERVICE ANALYSIS

A. Description

1. Describe here what the product/service is and what it does:

B. Comparison

1. What advantages does our product/service have over those of the competition (consider such things as unique features, patents, expertise, special training, etc.)?

2. What disadvantages does it have?

C. Some Consideration

1. Where will you get your materials and supplies?

2. List other considerations:

____

____

III. MARKETING STRATEGIES—MARKET MIX

A. Image

1. What kind of image do we want to have (such as cheap-but-good, or exclusive, or customer-oriented, or highest quality, or convenient, or speedy, or . . .)?

____

B. Features

1. List the features we will emphasize:

a. ____

b. ____

c. ____

C. Pricing

1. We will be using the following pricing strategy:

a. Markup on cost ______________

What % markup? ______________

b. Suggested price ______________

c. Is it competitive? ______________

d. Below competition ______________

e. Premium price ______________

f. Other ______________

2. Are our prices in line with our image?

YES __________ NO__________

3. Do our prices cover costs and leave a margin of profit?

YES __________ NO__________

D. Customer Services

1. List the customer services we provide:
   a. ______________________________
   b. ______________________________
   c. ______________________________
2. These are our sales/credit terms:
   a. ______________________________
   b. ______________________________
   c. ______________________________
3. The competition offers the following services:
   a. ______________________________
   b. ______________________________
   c. ______________________________

E. Advertising/Promotion

1. These are the things we wish to say about the business:

   ____

   ____

   ____
2. We will use the following advertising/promotion sources:
   a. Television ____________
   b. Radio ____________
   c. Direct Mail ____________
   d. Personal contacts ____________
   e. Trade associations ____________
   f. Newspapers ____________
   g. Magazines ____________
   h. Yellow Pages ____________
   i. Billboards ____________

   Other ______________________________

3. The following are the reasons we consider the media we have chosen to be the most effective:

____

____

____

MARKETING TIPS, TRICKS & TRAPS

1. Marketing Steps
   - Classifying your customers' needs
   - Targeting your customers
   - Examining your "niche"
   - Identifying your competitors
   - Assessing and managing your available resources
     —Financial
     —Human
     —Material
     —Production

2. Marketing Position
   - Follower versus leader
   - Quality versus price
   - Innovator versus adaptor
   - Service versus product
   - International versus domestic
   - Private sector versus government

3. Sales Strategy
   - Use customer-oriented selling approach—by getting agreement.
   - Phase 1: Establish rapport with customer—by agreeing to discuss what the customer wants to achieve.

     Phase 2: Determine customer objective—by agreeing on what the customer wants to achieve and those factors in the environment that will influence these results.

Phase 3: Recommend a customer action plan—by agreeing that using your product/service will indeed achieve customer wants.

Phase 4: Obtaining customer commitment—by agreeing that the customer will acquire your product/service.

- Emphasize Customer Advantage
  Must read:
  When a competitive advantage cannot be demonstrated, it will not translate into a benefit.
  Must be important to the customer:
  When the perception of competitive advantage varies between supplier and customer, the customer wins.
  Must be specific:
  When a competitive advantage lacks specificity, it translates into mere puffery and is ignored.
  Must be promotable:
  When a competitive advantage is proven, it is essential that your customer know it, or it doesn't truly exist.

4. Benefits vs. Features
   - The six "O's" of organizing customer buying behavior

ORIGINS of purchase	(Who buys it?)
OBJECT of purchase	(What do they need/buy?)
OCCASIONS of purchase	(When do they buy it?)
OUTLETS of purchase	(Where do they buy it?)
OBJECTIVES of purchase	(Why do they buy it?)
OPERATIONS of purchase	(How do they buy it?)

   - Sales maxim:
     "Unless the proposition appeals to their INTEREST, unless it satisfies their DESIRE, and unless it shows them a GAIN—then they will not buy!"

- Quality customer leads:

Level of need	Ability to pay
Authority to pay	Accessibility
Sympathetic attitude	Business history
One-source buyer	Reputation (price or quality)

- Convert features to benefits using the "which means" transition

CHAPTER SEVEN

Financial Management Plan

Chapter Chart

The financial plan is where everything comes together. Each decision you made while developing your business plan will be reflected in the financial plan. The financial plan includes income-expense projections, balance sheets, cash requirements, working capital needs and the total start-up capital required to get your business off the ground. This chapter will explain the different types of financial statements needed and why they are important to your success.

- The income statement will give you an idea of how much profit you can expect from your operation. The income will be the result of your marketing and pricing strategies. The expenses are the result of your operational plans and physical facility needs.
- The balance sheet presents your business's net worth year to year. This net worth is what will generate income for you and your family in the future.
- How you decide to obtain your start-up capital affects your net worth and financial performance ratios. More debt will result in interest expense. The sale of stock will require you to share ownership and decision making. These and other factors must be thoroughly analyzed to make the correct financial decisions.

FINANCIAL MANAGEMENT PLAN

Where the Rubber Meets the Road

The financial management plan is considered by some experts to be the single most critical section of a comprehensive business plan. It is certain that your business plan is not complete without one. How do you know if you have enough capital to start your business without an accurate estimate in the financial plan? How can you know if you need outside funding or loans without thorough analysis in the financial plan? How do you expect to be able to borrow money from a lender or convince a friend or relative to invest in your business, if you cannot show them that you know exactly what you are doing, how much money you need, when they can expect to be repaid or what their return on investment will be? Without a thorough, detailed, accurate financial management plan, your odds are not very good. Remember also that one of the biggest causes of management failures in small business is undercapitalization. Undercapitalization results from underestimating the amount of capital that is required when you develop your financial plan.

When it comes time to borrow money, your business and financial plans will be the criteria by which the lenders evaluate your business and ability to repay. Lenders will look for a number of basic factors in your plan. These factors will in all likelihood make or break your case. Understanding these basic financing issues is the first step in determining whether you need, are eligible to apply for, or qualify for a loan or financial assistance.

1. EQUITY INVESTMENT

Determining whether the company's level of debt is appropriate requires an analysis of the company's expected earnings and the variability of these earnings, as well as the ratio between total debt and equity. Strong equity and low debt levels provide resiliency which will help a firm weather periods of operational adversity. There must be careful examination of the debt-to-worth ratio of a company. Sufficient equity is particularly important to new businesses. Business loan applicants must have a reasonable amount invested to ensure that, along with any borrowed funds, the business can operate on a sound basis. A strong equity position ensures that owners will remain committed to their business.

2. EARNINGS REQUIREMENTS

Financial obligations are paid with cash, not profits. When cash outflow exceeds cash inflow for an extended period of time, a business cannot continue to operate. As a result, cash management is extremely important. In order to adequately support a company's operation, cash must be at the right place, at the right time, and in the right amount. A company must be able to meet debt payments as they come due.

3. WORKING CAPITAL

Working capital is the excess of current assets over current liabilities. Because working capital is the excess of the more liquid working assets over the firm's obligations that are due within one year, it measures the funds available to finance a company's current requirements and represents the cushion or margin of protection for a company's short-term creditors. Working capital is essential for a company to meet the continuous operational needs of doing business. The adequacy of working capital directly influences the firm's ability to meet its trade and short-term debt obligations, and ultimately its ability to remain financially viable.

4. COLLATERAL

To the extent that worthwhile assets are available, adequate collateral is usually required as security on most loans, including SBA guaranteed loans. However, an SBA loan generally will not be declined where inadequacy of collateral is the only unfavorable factor. In the event real estate is to be used as collateral, borrowers should be aware that banks and other regulated lenders are now required by law to obtain third-party appraisals on real estate related transactions of $50,000 or more. Certified appraisals are required for loans of $250,000 or more. When commercial real estate represents the major piece of collateral for a loan, the SBA will require a third-party appraisal.

Owner-occupied residences are generally used for collateral when:

1. The participating lender requires the residence as collateral.
2. The equity in the residence is substantial and other credit factors are weak.
3. Such collateral is necessary to assure that the principal(s) remain committed to the success of the venture for which the loan is being made.
4. The applicant operates the business out of the residence or other buildings located on the same parcel of land.

5. RESOURCE MANAGEMENT

The ability of a potential borrower to manage resources is a prime consideration when determining whether a loan will be made, and in what amount. Managerial capacity is an important factor involving such areas as education, experience and motivation. Proven ability in resource management is also a large consideration. Mathematical calculations based on information provided in financial statements show how resources have been managed in the past. It is important to understand that no single ratio will provide a complete illustration, but that several used in conjunction with one another will give an overall picture of management performance.

FINANCIAL STATEMENTS

Now that you have an understanding of the basic financial issues, it is hoped you will have the insight necessary to develop a sound financial plan.

A never-ending complaint we hear from accountants, bankers, franchisors and other professional groups you are critically dependent on, is that too many entrepreneurs do not fully understand financial statements. This seems to be particularly true when it comes to the income statement and balance sheet. Without understanding these figures, the business owner is often misled as to the actual net worth or value of the business and the amount of profit or loss. Although you can certainly ask an accountant for a full explanation, you should learn to know by yourself what these numbers tell you.

It is hoped that the material in this chapter will help move you towards that goal.

According to Ms. Linda DeMarlor, CPA and president of Taxmasters (301-230-0200), the financial statements that should be included in your financial section are:

1. Statement of start-up capital—estimates
2. Income statement—projections
3. Monthly cash flow—projections
4. Balance sheet—projections

In addition, top quality financial plans will also include copies of any loan applications you've filed, a capital equipment and supply list, a lease-hold improvements list and any other supporting documentation that would help explain to a lender the basis for your numbers.

As we discussed in the Business Plan chapter, the first step to building a sound financial plan is to develop a start-up budget based on realistic inputs from suppliers and service providers on the actual amount of money needed to open your business (start-up costs) and the amount needed to keep it open (operating costs).

There are two types of start-up expenses. First, there are recurring expenses. These are expense items you will need to fund from start-up capital (since no profits will be available yet) that will be ongoing and recurring every week or month or period. Some examples of recurring start-up expenses are:

- insurance
- legal/professional fees
- licenses/permits
- salaries/wages
- payroll expenses
- supplies
- utilities
- accounting

The second type of start-up expenses are one-time expenses. These are different from all other expenses in that they occur only once during the lifetime of the business and they occur during the start-up. They do not recur like salary or utilities. Examples of start-up expenses are:

- design of logo/stationery
- grand opening expenses
- licenses/permits
- site location expense
- equipment purchases
- leasehold improvements
- security deposits
- training

One important element of start-up expenses that is frequently overlooked is some level of working capital. Even though the plan is to fund future monthly expenses from profits and cash flow, we must include in our start-up capital enough money to cover all operating expenses in the event that a profit or surplus cash flow does not materialize as planned. For example, you might want to have a capital reserve equivalent to three to six months' worth of operating expenses in the event that it takes that long to earn a profit. You do not want to get into a situation where you have to close up shop after all your hard work because you have run out of money.

Statement of Start-Up Capital

Basic one-time costs

Real estate deposit . . . . ______

Phone deposit . . . . ______

Other utility deposits . . . . ______

Rent before opening . . . . ______

Phone before opening . . . . ______

Other utilities before opening . . . . ______

Payroll before opening . . . . ______

Remodeling costs . . . . ______

Equipment costs . . . . ______

Fixtures, furniture, signs . . . . ______

Legal fees . . . . ______

Accounting fees . . . . ______

Subtotal ______

Starting inventory/raw goods

Detail: ______ ______

______ ______

______ ______

Subtotal ______

Initial advertising/promotion

Detail: ______ ______

______ ______

______ ______

Subtotal ______

Reserve for months' operating expenses

Detail: ______ ______

______ ______

______ ______

Subtotal ______

TOTAL ______

INCOME STATEMENT—Projection

The income projections (profit and loss) statement is valuable both as a planning tool and a key management tool to help control business operations. It enables the owner-manager to develop a preview of the amount of income generated each month and for the business year, based on reasonable predictions of monthly levels of sales, costs and expenses—in other words, a budget.

As monthly projections are developed and entered into the income projections statement, they can serve as specific goals for controlling the business operation. As actual operating results become known each month, they should be recorded for comparison with the monthly projections. A completed income statement allows the owner-manager to compare actual figures with monthly projections and to take steps to correct any problems.

On the next page, a typical income statement is shown. It should be mentioned that there are sometimes differences in the income statement line items for certain industries. This is particularly evident in banks, loan companies and manufacturers. If you are considering a business in one of these industries, or if the general form of income statement does not seem correct, then you should consult with an accountant for advice. If you prefer, the information is readily available in any county or college library.

Income Statement—Projection

	Jan	Feb	Mar	Apr	May	Jun	Jul	Aug	Sep	Oct	Nov	Dec	Yearly	% of Revenue	Industry Avg. %
Total Revenue															
Costs of sales															
Gross profit															
Gross profit margin															
Controllable expenses															
Salaries/wages															
Payroll expenses															
Legal/accounting															
Advertising															
Automobile															
Office supplies															
Dues/subscriptions															
Utilities															
Misc.															
Total controllable exp															
Fixed expenses															
Rent															
Depreciation															
Utilities															
Insurance															
License/permits															
Loan payments															
Misc.															
Total fixed expenses															
Total expenses															
Net profit before taxes															
Taxes (state & fed.)															
Net profit after taxes															

Explanation of Terms

TOTAL REVENUES

Determine the total number of units of products or services you realistically expect to sell each month at the prices you expect to get. Use this step to create the projections to review your pricing practices.

- What returns, allowances and markdowns can be expected?
- Exclude any revenue that is not strictly related to the business.

COSTS OF SALES

The key to calculating your cost of sales is that you do not overlook any costs that you have incurred. Calculate cost of sales of all products and services used to determine total revenue. Where inventory is involved, do not overlook transportation costs. Also include any direct labor.

Income Statement Annual by Month

For Year: ________	Jan	Feb	Mar	Apr	May	June	July	Aug	Sept	Oct	Nov	Dec	Total
INCOME													
Gross Sales													
Less returns and allowances													
Net sales													
Cost of goods													
GROSS PROFIT													
OPERATING EXPENSES													
Sales expenses													
Commissions													
Marketing													
Total sales expenses													
General and administrative expenses Salaries and wages													
Employee benefits													
Professional services													
Rent													
Insurance													
Depreciation and amortization													
Office supplies													
Interest													
Telephone and utilities													
Postage													
Travel and entertainment													
Payroll taxes													
Maintenance													
Equipment rental													
Furniture and equipment													
Other													
Total G & A expenses													
TOTAL OPERATING EXPENSES													
Net income before taxes													
Taxes on income													
NET INCOME AFTER TAXES (NET PROFIT)													

Estimated Monthly Expenses

Item	Your estimate of monthly expenses based on sales of $__________ per year	Your estimate of how much cash you need to start your business (see column 3)	What to put in column 2 (These figures are typical for one kind of business. You will have to decide how many months to allow for in your business.)
	Column 1	Column 2	Column 3
Salary of owner-manager	$	$	3 times column 1
All other salaries and wages			3 times column 1
Rent			3 times column 1
Advertising			3 times column 1
Delivery expense			3 times column 1
Supplies			3 times column 1
Telephone and telegraph			3 times column 1
Other utilities			3 times column 1
Insurance			Payment required by insurance company
Taxes, including Social Security			4 times column 1
Interest			3 times column 1
Maintenance			3 times column 1
Legal and other professional fees			3 times column 1
Miscellaneous			3 times column 1
Starting costs you have to pay only once			Leave column 2 blank
Fixtures and equipment			Talk it over with suppliers
Decorating and remodeling			Talk it over with a contractor
Installation of fixtures and equipment			Talk to suppliers from whom you buy these
Starting inventory			Suppliers will probably help you estimate this
Deposits with public utilities			Find out from utility companies
Legal and other professional fees			Lawyer, accountant, and so on
Licenses and permits			Find out from city offices what you need to have
Advertising and promotion for opening			Estimate what you'll use
Accounts receivable			What you need to buy more stock until credit customers pay
Cash			For unexpected expenses or losses, special purchases, etc.
Other			Make a separate list and enter total
Total estimated cash you need to start			Add up all the numbers in column 2

GROSS PROFIT

Subtract the total cost of sales from the total revenue to obtain gross profit.

GROSS PROFIT MARGIN

The gross profit margin is expressed as a percentage of total revenues. It is calculated by dividing gross profits by total revenue.

CONTROLLABLE EXPENSES

These expenses are typically those that you have reasonable control over. They typically will include the expenses below.

- Salary expenses—Base pay plus overtime.
- Payroll expenses—Paid vacations, sick leave, health insurance, unemployment insurance and social security taxes.
- Outside services—Subcontracts, overflow work and special or one-time services.
- Supplies—Services and items purchased for use in the business.
- Repair/Maintenance—Regular maintenance and repair, including periodic large expenditures such as painting.
- Advertising—Desired sales volume and classified directory advertising expenses.
- Car delivery and travel—Charges if personal car is used in business, including parking, tools, buying trips, etc.
- Accounting and legal—Outside professional services.

FIXED EXPENSES

Fixed expenses are those which are basically a fixed amount per period. They usually include:

- Rent—Only real estate used in business.
- Depreciation—Amortization of capital assets.
- Utilities—Water, heat, light, etc.
- Insurance—Fire or liability on property or products. Include workers' compensation.
- Loan repayments—Interest on outstanding loans.

- Miscellaneous—Unspecified; small expenditures without separate accounts.
- License/permits—Any federal, state or local licenses or permits that are required.

NET PROFIT (LOSS) BEFORE TAXES
Subtract total expenses from gross profit.

TAXES
In addition to federal and state income taxes also include inventory and sales tax, excise tax, real estate tax, etc.

NET PROFIT (LOSS) AFTER TAXES
This is the amount of money that your company has made by doing business. It should be pointed out that this is after you have taken your own salary out of the business. To calculate, subtract taxes from net profit (before taxes).

ANNUAL TOTAL
For each of the sales and expense items in your income projection statement, add all the monthly figures across the table and put the result in the annual total column.

ANNUAL PERCENTAGE
Calculate the annual percentage by dividing the annual total by the total annual revenue. Compare this figure to the industry percentage in the last column to see how your business and management skills compare to the rest of the industry.

INDUSTRY PERCENTAGE
In the industry percentage column, enter the percentages of total revenues that are standard for your industry. They are derived by dividing each line item annual total by the total annual revenue.

Industry figures serve as a useful benchmark against which to compare cost and expense estimates that you develop for your firm. Compare the figures in the industry percentage column to those in the annual percentage column.

These percentages can be obtained from various sources, such as trade associations, accountants or banks. The reference librarian in your nearest public library can also refer you to documents that contain the percentage figures, for example, Robert Morris Associates' Annual Statement Studies (One Liberty Place, Philadelphia, PA 19103).

MONTHLY CASH FLOW STATEMENT—Projections

The monthly cash flow statement shows the projected and/or actual cash amount available during each time period, preferrably each month. This is the cash you will have available to pay bills and salaries, to purchase inventory, to pay rent and all the other expense items that require cash or checks to be disbursed. The bottom line, "Cash-on-Hand," is therefore the net difference between your receipts (what you take in) and your expenses (what you pay out). At first glance, the cash flow statement might look exactly like the income statement. However, there are some very important differences.

First, the income statement shows profits before and after taxes. It is, in addition to a statement of the condition of your business, a tax reporting vehicle. Your company is taxed on its net income. You will notice therefore that the income statement includes depreciation. Depreciation from a cash flow standpoint is not a real cash disbursement. It is an artificial expense created from the tax laws. Unless you have set up an account where this money must be placed each month for the purpose of replacing equipment in the future, there is no real cash impact.

Second, the cash flow statement measures only monies received. If your customers pay you every 60 or 90 days, then although you may have revenue (an income statement item) during the period, you will not have any cash until it is received by your company. Therefore, the cash flow statement will reflect your business policies on payment.

Third, since you may also pay your suppliers or payroll every 60 or 90 days, likewise, the cash flow statement would show no cash disbursements until you actually write the checks. Again, you would not show anything on the cash flow statement until that point.

You should be sure to understand the major point of this discussion. You may have plenty of sales or revenue on the books, but unless you have received the money you cannot pay your bills. Frequently, this is actually the cause of many bankruptcy filings. Companies with plenty of assets, a high net worth or stockholders' equity, but no cash to make the mortgage payments, frantically file for protection under the bankruptcy laws.

In summary, when projecting your cash flow, only show cash-in when you are planning on receiving it. Similarly, only show cash-out when you are planning on writing a check. An example of a typical cash flow statement appears below. For additional help, you should contact your accountant or take advantage of the resources at the SBA. There are several methods available to set up this statement, and you should be sure to enlist the help of the experts.

	January	February	March	April	May
Cash In					
Beginning cash					
Cash sales					
Receivables: 75%					
20%					
5%					
Lines of credit					
Other cash receipts					
Total Cash In					
Cash Outlays					
Rent					
Loan payments					
Payroll					
Interest					
Cost of goods sold					
Other expenses					
Total Cash Outlay					
Cash on Hand					

Items You Will Need To Develop The Cash Flow Statement

1. Total cash received each month. This amount includes all sources of money each month. It includes cash sales, collections from other periods, receivables from other periods, money that you borrow, lines of credit that you have established, income from investments or rent, sales of equity, and any other source of money.
2. Amount or percentage of credit sales and the pattern of collections. For example, 75% of your sales may be paid for in the following month, 20% paid for in the second month, and 5% paid for in the third month or not at all.
3. Payments you normally make as they occur each month. These usually include rent, payments of debt, royalties, interest, payroll, CODs, petty cash, and other non-invoiced charges.
4. The cost of goods sold plus other invoiced charges. These may include legal and accounting services, supplies, small equipment and miscellaneous charges.
5. Your payment patterns. You may find variation in these patterns based on the types of payables. For example, you may pay for goods or materials for sale within 30 days, but legal, accounting or other supplies frequently are not paid until 45 days after billing.

To illustrate how this statement is used, assume that your sales in January totalled $85,000, of which $45,000 was in cash and $40,000 was on credit. Your previous collection experience indicates that you will collect 75% of your receivables in 30 days, 20% within 60 days, and 5% within 90 days. You pay your vendors within 30 days but often let some other debtors go until 45 days. Now track January's transactions according to the preceding patterns. Cash sales are posted in January, the month received. Credit sales are receivables; consequently, 75% is projected to come in during February, 20% in March, and 5% in April. Your standard costs are those you pay during the month incurred; therefore they would be posted in January. You pay your vendors within 30 days (in February) but your other invoiced charges will be paid in March. By adding additional columns, you can show actual versus projected on the one table. If cash is tight, this statement can be of immense value.

BALANCE SHEETS

The balance sheet shows the company's financial condition at a specific period in time. Although this report is usually rendered at the end of the fiscal year, it can be prepared at any time.

At the top of the page fill in the legal name of the business, the type of statement and the day, month and year.

BALANCE SHEET

YOUR COMPANY NAME

As of ______________________________, 19____

ASSETS		**LIABILITIES**	
CURRENT ASSETS		CURRENT LIABILITIES	
Cash	$	Accounts payable	$
Petty cash	$	Notes payable	$
Accounts receivable	$	Interest payable	$
Inventory	$	Taxes payable	$
Short-term investment	$	State income tax	$
Prepaid expenses	$	Self-employment tax	$
TOTAL CURRENT ASSETS	$	Sales tax (SBE)	$
		Property tax	$
		Property tax	$
FIXED ASSETS		Federal income tax	$
Land	$	Payroll accrual	$
Buildings	$	TOTAL CURRENT LIABILITIES	$
Improvements	$		
Equipment	$	LONG-TERM LIABILITIES	
Furniture	$	Notes payable	$
Automobile/vehicles	$	TOTAL LONG-TERM LIABILITIES	$
OTHER ASSETS		TOTAL LIABILITIES	$
Long-term Investments	$	NET WORTH	
1.	$	Stockholder's equity	$
2.	$	Corporation capital stock	$
TOTAL FIXED/OTHER ASSETS	$	Surplus paid in	$
		Retained earnings	$
		TOTAL NET WORTH	$
TOTAL ASSETS	**$**	**TOTAL LIABILITIES+NET WORTH**	**$**

Note: Total assets must always equal total liabilities plus total net worth.

ASSETS

List anything of value that is owned or legally due the business.

1. *Current assets:* Cash and resources that can be converted into cash within 12 months of the date of the balance sheet (or during one established cycle of operation). Include money on hand and demand deposits in the bank, e.g., checking accounts and regular savings accounts.
    a. Petty cash: If your business has a fund for small miscellaneous expenditures, include the total here.
    b. Accounts receivable: The amounts due from customers in payment for merchandise or services.
    c. Inventory: Include raw materials on hand, work in progress and all finished goods, either manufactured or purchased for resale.
    d. Short-term investments: Also called temporary investments or marketable securities, these include interest- or dividend-yielding holdings expected to be converted into cash within a year. List stocks and bonds, certificates of deposit and time-deposit savings accounts at either their costs or market value, whichever is less.
    e. Prepaid expenses: Goods, benefits or services a business buys or rents in advance. Examples are office supplies, insurance protection and floor space.
2. *Long-term investments:* Also called long-term assets, these are holdings the business intends to keep for at least a year and that typically yield interest or dividends. Included are stocks, bonds and savings accounts earmarked for special purposes.
3. *Fixed assets:* Also called plant and equipment. Includes all resources a business owns or acquires for use in operations and not intended for resale. Fixed assets may be leased. Depending on the leasing arrangements, both the value and the liability of the leased property may need to be listed on the balance sheet.
    a. Land: List original purchase price without allowances for market value.

b. Buildings, improvements, equipment, furniture, automobile/ vehicles: Value shown is purchase price minus depreciation.

4. *Total assets include all net values:* These are the amounts derived when you subtract depreciation and amortization from the original costs of acquiring the assets.

LIABILITIES

Anything that is owed to any person or institution or government agency.

1. *Current liabilities:* List all debts, monetary obligations and claims payable within 12 months or within one cycle of operation. Typically they include the following:
   a. Accounts payable—Amounts owed to suppliers for goods and services purchased in connection with business operations.
   b. Notes payable—The balance of principal due to pay off short-term debt for borrowed funds.
   c. Interest payable—Any accrued fees due for use of both short- and long-term borrowed capital and credit extended to the business.
   d. Taxes payable—Amounts estimated by an accountant to have been incurred during the accounting period.
   e. Payroll accrual—Salaries and wages currently owed.

2. *Long-term liabilities:* List notes, contract payments or mortgage payments due over a period exceeding 12 months or one cycle of operation. They are listed by outstanding balance less the current position due. Typically they include:
   a. Notes payable—Money owed which is greater than 1 but less than 10 years in term.
   b. Bonds or Mortgage—Money owed which is greater than 10 years in term.

NET WORTH

Also called owner's equity, net worth is the claim of the owner(s) on the assets of the business. In a proprietorship or partnership, equity is each owner's original investment plus any earnings after withdrawals.

TOTAL LIABILITIES AND NET WORTH

The sum of these two amounts must always match that of total assets.

CHAPTER EIGHT

How To Structure Your Business

The Key To Your Survival and Financial Independence

Chapter Chart

Which form of business ownership is right for you? It's an important question, since the alternatives affect every aspect of your business. This chapter presents the major forms of business ownership and explanations of the positives and negatives of each.

- Sole proprietorships give you maximum control of your business but leave you personally liable for bills and damages incurred by the company.
- Partnerships offer better chances of liability protection and spread the risk among the partners. They, however, could leave you open to power struggles, in-fighting and other personal problem areas of conflict.
- Corporations minimize the problems of the other two forms but they are more costly to set up and run. There are formalities you must follow if you want to maintain the liability protection.
- Limited liability companies (LLCs), a relatively new form of business organization, is a combination partnership and corporation. It has been called by experts, "The Organizational Form of the Next Century."

How To Structure Your Business

Sole Proprietorship, Corporation, Partnership or Limited Liability Company (LLC)

So, you have chosen a product, a service or an idea to develop. You know how to make the items or perform the service. The next issue that must be decided is to choose the correct legal structure or business entity for your business. Whichever option you choose will have a significant impact on your journey along the road to profits, financial independence and wealth.

What is a business entity? A business entity is a legal association or statutory creation. In other words, a particular state's laws and statutes define and authorize the various types of business entities. It is these statutes that define the limits of liability and the formalities that must be followed. However, it should be understood that it is the IRS that dictates tax regulations. The states pass laws defining and permitting business entities. The IRS will then determine how to tax them.

There are several alternate structures from which to choose. There are forms of doing business that are fairly well known and common; namely, sole proprietorship, corporation, general partnership, and limited partnership. There is a new alternative, now available in about 40 states, called a limited liability company (LLC). Finally, there are a few exotic options, relatively unknown and infrequently used, like the business trust, nonprofit corporation, etc. Because of the nature of these alternatives, they should probably be avoided for most boot camp entrepreneurs, and they will not be addressed in this chapter.

The choice you make will directly affect income taxes and personal liability. There are, in addition, many other factors to be considered. The table following lists many of the issues; however, taxes and liability are the two most critical elements. These two factors alone could make the difference between financial health and financial sickness or death.

FACTORS AFFECTING THE CHOICE OF BUSINESS ORGANIZATION

1. Taxation
2. Liability
3. Legal restrictions
4. Nature of operations
5. Need for capital
6. Division of earnings
7. Number of people involved
8. Endurance of the business

Income Taxation. As a result of changes introduced in federal income tax legislation, the top tax bracket for a married couple is now 39.6%. When adjustments are made to this bracket for the deductions lost at higher income levels, the effective maximum federal tax bracket climbs to an unbelievable 42.4%. And on top of this you must add a state income tax of maybe 5 or 6%, bringing the bottom-line total to almost 50%. That's right, almost 50% of your hard-earned money is paid to Uncle Sam in the way of taxes. Obviously, the tax your business pays reduces your wealth, but in addition, these taxes also affect your competitiveness. If you can pay less tax than your competition, then you can lower your prices and capture more market share. It is therefore our opinion that income tax planning is the single most important factor in the choice of business form. Although liability is of major importance also, we can solve this problem many ways with just about any option chosen. The decision process should be, first, choose the entity that results in the least overall family taxes; second, decide how to protect against liability claims.

Liability. Ms. Karin Dunlap, attorney-at-law (703-706-0213), estimates that last year approximately 20,000,000 lawsuits were filed in the U.S. This translates to about 55,000 per day and these numbers do not even include actions that were settled prior to a formal suit being filed. The bases for these suits are personal injury, wrongful termination, breach of contract, discrimination, etc. The fact is that the average person in business today will be sued **FIVE** times during the lifetime of their business. Even if you are innocent, you still must spend substantial sums of money to defend yourself—maybe $15,000 to $25,000. If you are found liable, the costs could be greater. Certainly, you can buy liability or errors and omissions insurance, and this is an excellent course to pursue. However, with the ever increasing size of jury awards, now in the tens of millions of dollars, you cannot afford enough insurance to protect your family's wealth. The form of business structure that you put in place must be chosen to protect your personal as well as your business assets. The question is no longer, "If I am sued," but "When I am sued." It is amazing, given the probability of litigation, that over 70% of all businesses in the country today have been organized as sole proprietorships.

Entity Integration. No matter what your current sources of income are, the business entities must be analyzed to determine how the new venture will integrate into your existing family financial structure. You cannot make an effective decision without studying how the new business's income, taxes, and liability will or can affect your current taxes and net worth.

If you already have substantial employment income or an existing business, you may not want the new business income to flow through to your personal tax return and push you into a higher tax bracket. If your hard work and sweat have successfully built a net worth of $100,000 or more, you might not want to jeopardize losing even a dime to a frivolous lawsuit. If the business is anticipated to initially lose money, it would be wise to structure yourself to use this loss to reduce your current income taxes. This is particularly beneficial in dual-income families. For these reasons and others, a comprehensive overall analysis must be made at the outset of your business to examine the effects the new venture will have.

SOLE PROPRIETORSHIP

"America's Traditional Form of Doing Business."

The sole proprietorship is America's traditional form of doing business. The term sole proprietorship means that the business is the same as its owners. The assets and liabilities of the business are one and the same as the owner. No entity is created; the business is destined to the same financial fate as the owner.

Profit or Loss. When you figure your personal taxable income for the year, you must add in any profit or subtract any loss you have from your sole proprietorship. You must report the profit or loss from each of your businesses operated as a sole proprietorship on a separate Schedule C (tax Form 1040) or Schedule C-EZ (tax Form 1040). The amount of this business profit or loss is then entered as an item of profit or loss on your individual tax return Form 1040.

If you are a sole proprietorship, you are probably liable for self-employment tax. Also, ordinarily you will have to make estimated tax payments.

Assets. Each asset in your sole proprietorship is treated separately for tax purposes, rather than as part of one overall ownership interest. For example, a sole proprietor selling an entire business as a going concern would figure gain or loss separately on each asset.

General Characteristics

- Approximately 70% of all U.S. businesses are sole proprietorships
- Legal basis—common law
- Limited life span—its life is limited to that of its owners; when the owner dies, the business dies
- Unlimited personal liability—the business is the same as the owner both legally and fiscally
- Owner operated—no board of directors, no stockholders, no partners
- Limited financing—must finance operations by borrowing money or reinvesting profits

Advantages

- No entity filing requirements—quick and inexpensive to start and get in operation
- Greatest freedom of action
- Simple to operate—owner makes all decisions

- May register a trade name—prevents confusion resulting from deceptively similar names
- No separate taxation—the owner pays all taxes personally
- Income tax advantage possible in very small firms
- Social Security advantages to the owner

Disadvantages

- Unlimited liability—if the business is sued so is the owner
- No continuity of life—if the owner dies or becomes incapacitated the business does not continue
- Limited financing—proprietorships raise money only by borrowing or dipping into savings
- Growth limited to personal energies
- Personal affairs too easily mixed with business affairs

Tax Implications

- Personal taxation—profits are taxed as personal income on IRS Form 1040, Schedule C
- Self employment tax—read IRS Publication 533 and use IRS Form SE
- Estimated tax payments—read IRS Publication 505
- Obtain IRS "Tax Guide for Small Business" by calling 1-800-829-3676

GENERAL PARTNERSHIPS

> ***"Give as much thought to picking your business partners as you would give to picking a spouse."***

A general partnership is an association of at least two persons who co-own a business. Partnerships are formed when two or more people, partnerships, corporations or associations desire to share ownership, management, profits and liabilities of a business venture. Partnerships may be formed by a contractual understanding between the parties and may be written in the form of "partnership agreements" or may be oral agreements. You may look at partnerships as separate entities because they may contract in their own name; may hold title to assets in their name; may be sued in their own name; must file income tax returns; and are recognized as entities by bankruptcy laws. Individual assets of partners may not be sheltered from judgments against the partnerships, so the partnership is not a true entity separate and apart from its owners.

Partnership agreement. The partnership agreement includes the original agreement and any modifications agreed to by all the partners or adopted in any other manner provided for by the partnership agreement. The agreement or modifications may be oral or written.

Generally, a partner's share of income, gain, loss, deductions or credits is determined by the partnership agreement. The partnership agreement may be modified for a particular tax year after the close of that year, but not later than the date, excluding any extension of time, for filing the partnership return. However, if the modification made does not produce substantial economic effects, it could be disregarded.

Partnerships excluded. If all members agree, some partnerships may choose to be completely or partially excluded from being treated as partnerships for federal tax purposes. The exclusion applies only to certain investing partnerships and operating agreements where business is not actively conducted. It applies to the joint production, extraction, or use of property, but not for selling services or property produced or extracted. The members of such an organization must be able to figure their income without having to figure partnership taxable income.

General Characteristics

- Quick and inexpensive to form—two or more persons may contract to form a partnership either by written or oral agreement. The agreements are not required to be filed
- Legal basis—express contract of owners or implied contract in law by the courts
- Not a separate entity—while partnerships may hold title or sue or file income tax returns, there is no limitation on liability accruing against individual partner assets

- Easy operation—any partner may make decisions without meetings or resolutions through sharing of management and profit
- Unlimited liability—any partner may bind all other partners jointly and individually. Each partner's individual assets may be sued to satisfy a judgment arising from the acts of any other partner
- Limited life—the partnership must be dissolved and reformed upon the death or incompetence of any partner
- Favorable taxation—partnership return is filed but profits and gains are not taxed to the partnership

Advantages

- Simple and inexpensive to form—no state, federal or local filings required
- Easy to operate—partners may make quick decisions without required meetings
- May register a trade name—prevents confusion resulting from deceptively similar business names
- No separate taxation—partners pay taxes for their share of partnership gains
- Quasi-entity—may own assets, contract in partnership name, may sue and be sued in partnership name
- Equal sharing of profit and management—profit divided according to agreement and each partner has management responsibilities

Disadvantages

- Unlimited liability—any partner is held absolutely liable individually for the acts of the partnership or any of the other partners
- No continuity of life—if any partner dies or becomes incompetent, the partnership must dissolve and be reformed
- Limited financing—may only borrow money or use partner's savings. Must be dissolved and reformed to admit additional partners wishing to invest
- Deadlock—partners may become deadlocked when decision making is split equally

Tax Implications

- Partnership files IRS Form 1065
- Partners pay tax—each partner receives a K-1 which shows the distributive share of partnership items to be declared on partner's 1040
- Estimated tax payments—may be subject to quarterly tax payments. See IRS Publication 505
- Social Security—partners may be subject to self-employment tax. See IRS Publication 533
- Read IRS Publication 541 on partnerships
- Obtain "Tax Guide for Small Business" by calling 1-800-829-3676

LIMITED PARTNERSHIPS

"Not just for tax shelters."

Limited partnerships are formed by at least one general partner and one limited partner who have filed their agreement with the Secretary of State. The general partner provides management and has individual liability. Limited partners take no part in management but supply capital and have liability limited to their original investment. Limited partnerships are useful for owning expensive assets, owning property or raising capital. Limited partnerships file a "Certificate of Limited Partnership" with the Secretary of State and may have to register the limited partnership interests as securities with the Secretary of State. People involved in such activities as leasing and real estate investment and medical technology investment have used limited partnerships as entities to operate their businesses.

General Characteristics

- Formation—every limited partnership must be formed in writing between at least one general partner and at least one limited partner and be filed with the Secretary of State
- Legal basis—statutes of each state

- General partners—manage the enterprise and have unlimited liability for all partnership debts
- Limited partners—must not manage in any capacity and have liability limited to their individual investments
- Tax benefits—the limited partnership files a return, but its general partner and limited partners pay the taxes individually
- Specific time period—while statutes do not mandate limited life, a limited partnership for tax reasons is normally formed for a specified time period, not in perpetuity

Advantages

- Limited liability—investors have liability limited to their respective investments in the partnership
- Separate entity—may sue and be sued, own property, protect its limited partners from unlimited liability, may raise capital by selling interests in the partnership, borrow money and exist independently of its partners' mortality
- Not mortal—does not have to be dissolved and reformed every time a general partner or limited partner dies
- Capital generation—may borrow money or use general partner savings, funds from operations, sales of limited partner interests
- Management authority—managed by the general partner and not subject to investor interference
- Tax advantage—partnership does not pay tax; profits and losses pass through the entity to the partners

Disadvantages

- Complicated accounting—a limited partnership requires advanced accounting procedures
- Limited life—does not live in perpetuity, but lives for a stipulated period, usually for the life of the asset it owns
- Lack of control—limited partners have little voice in management once the investment is made in the partnership
- Securities laws—if more than 15 partners are involved (varies by state) or if sales commissions are given for selling the interests, the limited partnership must register its securities before they are sold

- Non-liquid investment—interests may not be freely traded; therefore, a limited partner must hold the investment indefinitely
- Expensive to form and operate—a written agreement must be filed with the Secretary of State, annual financial reporting to limited partners, and accounting for all moneys received and disbursed

Tax Implications

- Personal taxation—the partnership files an IRS Form 1065 but individual partners pay taxes on their share of profits shown on K-1s via Form 1040
- Tax identification number—the partnership must apply for and receive a tax identification number
- Partnership taxation—IRS Publication 541 explains taxation and forms
- Estimated tax—IRS Publication 505 explains the need for estimating and prepaying taxes
- Self-employment tax—IRS Publication 533 addresses need for general partner self-employment withholding
- Obtain "Tax Guide for Small Business" by calling 1-800-829-3676

CORPORATIONS

"The workhorse of American business."

As mentioned previously, business entities are defined by statutes and their respective taxation is governed by IRS regulations. As such, there are several statutory classifications and tax classifications of corporations. The most common statutory classifications are for-profit, stock corporations and close corporations. There are other possibilities, such as professional corporations and non-profit corporations. They will not be discussed since they have less general applicability.

The basic tax classifications of corporations are a "C" corporation, the normal business corporation, and "S" corporation, a special case for smaller companies. The letter "C" or "S" refers to the subchapter in the IRS tax code that defines the tax regulations. As in the case of statutes, there are a few additional categories; namely, personal holding company and personal service corporation. These are special cases and considered outside the scope of this book.

The "C" and "S" corporations are the workhorse business entities, most commonly formed for raising capital and limiting individual liability. The corporation is a separate "legal person." It may live forever or be empowered to protect the shareholder from economic harm. It may own assets, sue or be sued, transfer its ownership easily, borrow money, mortgage its assets, and file bankruptcy. Corporations may also be held criminally responsible for illegal or unlawful activities. A board of directors and corporate officers remove day-to-day management from the hands of the owners (shareholders). Shareholders may elect the board at shareholder meetings. The board elects the corporate officers.

Taxation. Corporations pay taxes on annual profits. When the profits are distributed as dividends, the dividends are taxed to the shareholders. This double taxation of the profits is frequently one of the reasons people involved in small business avoid the corporate form.

In figuring its taxable income, a corporation generally takes the same deductions as a sole proprietorship. Corporations can also take advantage of special deductions that sole proprietorships cannot.

A corporation must file an income tax return unless it has dissolved. This applies even if it has ceased doing business and has disposed of all of its assets except a small sum of cash to pay state taxes to retain its corporate charter. A corporation without assets is not required to file an income tax return. Most corporations file Form 1120 or Form 1120-A.

Formation. To form a corporation, shareholders exchange money or property for stock in the corporation. If money or property is exchanged for stock, it is usually a nontaxable exchange. Care must be taken as unwanted taxable events could occur by mistake. To be sure, check with a competent accountant *before* the transfer.

General Characteristics

- Separate entity—a corporation is a separate entity formed to be and act as a legal person
- Easy transfer of ownership—merely by selling stock to new buyer
- Legal basis—state statutes
- Limited liability—owner shareholders are insulated from debts and liabilities of the corporation by state law. Certain provisions must be met
- Corporate articles—must be filed with the Secretary of State to form the entity
- Double taxation—corporate profits are taxed for the entity. Then money returned to owners as dividends, etc. is taxed as personal income
- Capital generation—may borrow money, issue bonds, sell common and preferred stock, enter into investment contracts
- Continuity of life—the entity may live forever without interruption by death of shareholders, directors, or officers

Advantages

- Limited liability—no shareholder, officer or director may be held liable for debts of the corporation unless corporate law was breached
- Capital generation—may sell common or preferred stock, issue bonds, borrow money, mortgage assets or contract for many types of financing
- Continuity of life—the entity exists forever so long as corporate regulations are met. No need to wind up operations if an owner or manager dies
- Ease of ownership transfer—the assets may be sold, transferred, pledged, or mortgaged simply by using stock
- Centralized management—practical control of business is performed by officers at the direction of the board of directors. Control is vested in majority ownership

Disadvantages

- More expensive to start and operate—corporate articles and amendments must be drafted and filed with the Secretary of State
- Double taxation—corporate profits are taxed for the entity and the return to investors, dividends, is taxed again to the individual
- Securities regulation—sales of bonds, notes, stock, investment contracts, etc. to raise money requires securities registration if more than 15 shareholders (varies by state) are approached or if a sales commission is paid to sell the stock
- Required meetings and reporting—statutes require meetings and shareholder reports
- Share ownership sales—ownership of the company is lost by selling shares of stock. Do not sell more than 49% ownership of the company
- Inflexible management—typically requires board action to make decisions, with a generous time lag
- Deadlock—shareholder and board of director disputes may disrupt decision-making process sufficiently to force court action, especially in family-owned corporations
- Since a corporation is a separate legal entity, any shareholders who also work for the corporation are employees for whom unemployment insurance taxes must be paid

Tax Implications

- Read IRS Publication 542 on corporate taxation
- Corporations file an IRS Form 1120 and report earnings and taxable profit
- May be subject to estimated tax payments (quarterly). Read IRS Publication 505
- May have to collect employee withholding
- Order "Tax Guide for Small Business" by calling 1-800-829-3676

CLOSE CORPORATIONS

"Typical private or family run corporation."

The close corporation was created by an act of legislature for small companies having just a few stockholders. These stockholders usually have ties to one another through family relationships or as friends and business partners. Close corporations are special cases of regular business corporations electing to operate in a more informal manner similar to partnerships. Regular business corporations must conduct shareholder and director meetings, elect a board of directors, and provide shareholders with written proposals for any major corporate action. The shareholders vote at annual meetings to disposition these proposals. Family corporations usually do not hold annual meetings because the family regularly makes decisions around the breakfast table or some equally informal setting. The close corporation law allows small corporations to forego some traditional corporate formalities.

General Characteristics

- Limited shareholders—corporations may have not more than 35 shareholders and still be a close corporation
- Legal basis—state statutes
- Special action necessary—the corporation becomes a close corporation by amending the articles of incorporation
- Abbreviated governance—shareholders may agree in writing to treat the corporation as a partnership, operate without a board of directors, dispense with annual meetings, and make a shareholder agreement

Advantages

- Limited liability—the law says shareholders don't have personal liability even though they relax corporate formalities in operations
- Ease of operations—operates without pomp and circumstance required in regular corporations where possibly hundreds of shareholders must receive information and vote

- Cost of operation—relaxed corporate governance means lower legal, accounting and administrative fees for lower total costs of operation
- Deadlock prevention—provides access to court when shareholders are deadlocked and harm could befall the corporation through lack of action
- Buy-out provisions—shareholders may buy out a deceased shareholder's interests according to shareholder agreements

Disadvantages

- Limited ownership transfer—share transfer prohibited except in stated circumstances
- Fewer capital sources—a close corporation is limited to 35 shareholders
- Expensive to form—forming the corporation and drafting a solid shareholder agreement is expensive and complicated
- Filings—every year a close corporation must file an annual report and pay annual report fees like any other corporation
- Double taxation—again, as in the case of a regular business corporation, profits are taxed to the corporation and the dividends are taxed to the individual

Tax Implications

- Same—close corporations are the same as regular corporations

"S" CORPORATIONS

"Special tax treatment for corporations."

A qualifying corporation may choose to be generally exempt from federal income taxes. Its shareholders will then include in their income their proportionate share of the corporation's income, deductions, etc. A corporation that makes this choice is called an "S" corporation.

Although it generally will not be liable for federal income tax, there are some unique situations when an "S" corporation may have to pay taxes. For example, an "S" corporation may be liable for capital gains taxes, a tax on passive income, a tax on built-in gains or the tax from re-computing a prior year's investment credit. An "S" corporation files its return on Form 1120S.

The IRS grants "S" status to any regular business corporation or close corporation that meets specific criteria. Ms. Judy Planzer, CPA and expert business consultant (301-858-7101) explains that in order to qualify for "S" status the corporation must have fewer than 35 shareholders, only one class of stock is permitted, and all shareholders must be U.S. citizens. All stockholders must pass a corporate resolution requesting "S" status from the IRS. In this way, all gains, losses, credits and deductions will be passed to the shareholders. "S" status avoids the corporate malady of "double taxation." Individual shareholders may benefit from a reduction in their taxable income if the corporation operates at a loss. Despite their unique tax treatment, "S" corporations maintain such full corporate attributes as limited liability and continuity of life. Whether a corporation is a regular "C" corporation or a close corporation, it may be an "S" corporation for tax purposes.

General Characteristics

- Limited shareholders—no more than 35 shareholders
- Domestic corporation—must be organized in the U.S.
- One class—must have only one class of common stock
- Citizen shareholders—must have shareholders who are residents of the U.S. and no nonresident alien shareholders
- Legal basis—IRS code and regulations
- Special action necessary—all shareholders must consent to "S" status
- Special action necessary—the IRS election is made by filing the IRS Form 2553. Read IRS Publication 589
- Tax advantage—small corporations may avoid double taxation by passing gains or losses on to the owner or shareholders

Advantages

- Corporate attributes—offers shareholders limited personal liability and offers the corporation continuity of life
- Tax advantage—corporate income tax payments are not required

- Early loss benefit—since corporations may operate at a loss in their first years, shareholders may benefit from a reduction in their personal taxable income by reporting their share of this loss on their personal taxes

Disadvantages

- Limited capital sources—may have 35 or fewer shareholders, thus limiting the ability to raise capital
- Class limitation—may not have debt convertible to stock or preferential rights to assets or profits that would create more than one class of stock
- Filings—requires IRS filings and additional accounting procedures
- Shareholder restrictions—foreigners, corporations and partnerships cannot be shareholders of an "S" corporation

LIMITED LIABILITY COMPANY

"The business structure of the '90s."

In 1977 a piece of special legislation was passed creating a unique entity called the Wyoming Limited Liability Company (LLC). It offers protection from personal liability as a corporation and receives the tax treatment of a limited partnership without any restrictions on citizenship or numbers of members. No general partner is liable for all debts of the enterprise. Each member of an LLC enjoys limited liability to that of the investment in the program and pays tax individually in proportion to ownership thus avoiding the corporate malady of double taxation. An IRS revenue ruling was received in 1988 stating that the Wyoming Limited Liability Company would be taxed as a partnership. Since that time, nearly 40 states have formulated statutes permitting LLCs.

General Characteristics

- Limited liability—each member enjoys limited liability up to the amount of capital invested

- Legal basis—state statute
- Tax advantage—avoids double taxation because its members pay taxes like partners in a partnership
- Limited life—must be formed for a period not exceeding 30 years, and must vote to continue upon the death of any member
- Nontransferable interest—a member may not transfer his or her voting interest without concurrence of all remaining members
- Name requirement—must contain the words "Limited Liability Company"
- Formation—must be formed by a written management agreement filed with the Secretary of State between two or more entities (people or organizations)

Advantages

- Limited liability—a creditor may not seek satisfaction of any LLC debt against the personal assets of any member of the LLC
- Tax advantage—the members each pay their share of tax in their share of the profits, avoiding double taxation of LLC profits
- Number of investors—may have any number of investors; not restricted to 35 like an "S" corporation
- No general partner—unlike the general partner in a limited partnership, the manager of an LLC does not have unlimited liability for debts and the manager need not maintain 1% interest in the entity

Disadvantages

- Limited transfer of interest—an investor is not liquid since all members must vote to transfer a member's interest
- Expensive to form and operate—complicated to form legally and requires substantial accounting work
- Not universally accepted—all states do not recognize LLCs
- Lack of case law—little guidance is provided by case law since this is an entity of recent creation and few cases have been brought to the courts

Tax Implications

- Treated as a limited partnership provided it also operates with centralized management and limited lifetime

THE REST OF THE STORY

We have tried in this chapter to present a description of the various options available to someone starting a business. But remember, there is a big difference between the needs of small, individually- or family-owned businesses and larger organizations. Much of what you read and much of the advice that you will get does not really mean much to small entrepreneurs. For example, let's discuss the disadvantages of incorporating listed above from the more pertinent viewpoint of someone wishing to own a small business.

Disadvantages

- *More expensive to start and operate*—this is in all likelihood a true statement; but, let's quantify "more expensive." Corporate articles and amendments must be drafted and filed with the Secretary of State. The state fees in most jurisdictions are $50 to $100. Most attorneys will draw up the articles of incorporation, bylaws, and handle all filings for less than $500. Or you can easily handle incorporating yourself, which will bring your total costs to less than $100. (The process for incorporating is detailed later on in this chapter.)
- *Double taxation*—corporate profits are taxed for the corporation and the return to investors, dividends, is taxed again to the individual. This is true; but you as the majority shareholder can elect not to distribute profits as dividends. There are many other ways to get the cash out of your corporation, e.g. loans, salary, etc. In fact, upon further thought and study, you will realize that there is no reason to take capital out of the corporate umbrella. You can purchase stock or bond investments from a corporate account. You can purchase rental real estate from your corporation. You can pay for your medical, dental, car and many other expenses using pre-tax dollars directly from your corporation. As a matter of fact, it might be advantageous to do so. There is

an 80% tax exclusion on dividends received by a corporation. You or I will pay taxes on 100% of the dividends. Of course, there are some rules about this, and your accountant or the IRS can explain them to you.

- *Securities regulation*—sales of bonds, notes, stock, investment contracts, etc., to raise money require securities registration if more than 15 shareholders (varies by state) are approached or if a sales commission is paid to sell the stock. This is really a "So what?" The reality is that this is an issue for less than 10% of all corporations in the country.
- *Required meetings and reporting*—statutes require meetings and shareholder reports. Again, true, but with word processors and computers, for many small businesses, this might constitute a few hours a year. For example, the requirement in most states is for a single annual stockholders' meeting.
- *Share ownership sales*—ownership of the company is lost by selling shares of stock. You should not sell more than 49% of the company. By the use of non-voting stock, you can actually sell or give away 99% of your stock and still keep total control.
- *Inflexible management*—typically requires board action to make decisions, with a generous time lag. Yes, but YOU are the board. How many times do you expect to reject your own proposals?
- *Deadlock*—shareholder and board of director disputes may disrupt decision-making process sufficiently to force court action, especially in family-owned corporations. Yes, again, but YOU are the board.

We hope you get the point!!! The reality is that by knowing your objectives and business requirements, the inner workings of corporations or partnerships, and your income tax particulars, and by knowing and utilizing experts, most if not all of the objections against corporations will probably vanish. When you consider the liability protection, the retirement benefits, the tax advantages and many other elements, there is little reason to be a sole proprietorship. The benefits of incorporation far outweigh any costs. The corporation is the workhorse of American business and the centerpiece for your financial plans.

An excellent book, and the only book of its kind in the country explaining the use and points of the corporation is *The Corporation Manual*. See Appendix Two, Recommended Resources, to get ordering information.

Let's take a closer look at the federal income tax picture. The tax regulations that became law in 1993 define the following tax brackets for married couples filing jointly and corporations.

As you can see from the table, at net profits of less than $100,000, federal income taxes for your business (exclusive of any salary and wages received by either spouse) would be less with a corporation. Between $100,000 and about $435,000 (not shown in table), a sole proprietorship would be the best option. And for all cases with net profits above $435,000, the statistics again favor the corporation.

According to Ms. Judy Planzer, a CPA and expert business consultant (301-858-7101), the vast majority of small businesses in America have net profits below the $100,000 level. You should keep in mind that this is $100,000 NET. That is after you have taken all the legal expense deductions in your corporations, after you have put up to $30,000 for you and/or your spouse into a pension plan, after you have purchased any corporate tax shelters, and after you have used fringe benefits like a health club on premises, day care, or medical and dental, etc. The point is that for most of us, the regular business C corporation is the way to go. Certainly it is hard to imagine many cases for the small entrepreneur where the net would be over $100,000. If you are fortunate enough to have higher profits, then you can always set up a new corporation.

You should always consult with a competent tax professional to ensure that you fully understand your actual or projected income taxes and plan accordingly.

If you would like assistance in structuring your business to propel you towards your goals of wealth and financial independence, our consultants at the National Management Center would be more than glad to assist you. **This is our business.** Please feel free to contact us at any time by calling 301-571-9480.

Married Filing Joint				"C" Corporations				Savings/Cost of "C" Corporation
From	To	Tax Rate	Tax Liability	From	To	Tax Rate	Tax Liability	
0	$ 36,900	15.0%	$ 5,535	**0**	**$ 36,900**	**15.0%**	**$ 5,535**	**0**
$ 36,901	$ 50,000	28.0%	$ 9,203	**$ 36,901**	**$ 50,000**	**15.0%**	**$ 7,500**	**$ 1,703**
$ 50,001	$ 75,000	28.0%	$ 16,203	**$ 50,001**	**$ 75,000**	**25.0%**	**$ 13,750**	**$2,453**
$ 75,001	$ 89,150	28.0%	$ 20,165	**$ 75,001**	**$ 89,150**	**34.0%**	**$ 18,561**	**$1,604**
$ 89,151	$ 100,000	31.0%	$ 23,528	**$ 89,151**	**$ 100,000**	**34.0%**	**$ 22,250**	**$ 1,278**
$100,001	**$140,000**	**31.0%**	**$ 35,929**	$ 100,001	$ 140,000	39.0%	$ 37,850	–$ 1,921
$140,001	**$250,000**	**36.0%**	**$ 75,529**	$ 140,001	$ 250,000	39.0%	$ 80,750	–$ 5,221
$250,001	**$335,000**	**39.6%**	**$109,189**	$ 250,001	$ 335,000	39.0%	$113,900	–$ 4,711
$335,000	above	39.6%		**$335,000**	**$10,000,000**	**34.0%**		

HOW TO INCORPORATE YOURSELF FOR FREE

(You will still need to pay the state filing fees.)

The process of incorporation is really quite straightforward. Simply by calling the Corporation Commission at the Secretary of State's office for your particular state, you can obtain instructions, all the forms that you will need, your articles of incorporation and other valuable information. It should be mentioned that a thorough study and analysis of how the business will fit into your family's existing financial infrastructure must be completed first. Then and only then, if a corporation is the proper solution, follow the steps below (or if you can afford it, contact an attorney).

1. Call the State Corporation Commission and ask them to send you the incorporation brochure and sample Articles of Incorporation.
2. Choose a name for your business. The name will have to include "Corp." or "Inc." as a suffix.
3. Call the Corporation Commission to see if the name is available. If so, ask them to reserve it for you.
4. Following the instructions in the material sent to you from the state, fill out the blank Articles of Incorporation and send them in with a check for the appropriate amount.
5. Once the Articles are returned to you by the state, call the IRS and obtain an EIN (Employer Identification Number).

You are now incorporated.

There are several additional formalities that must be followed to complete the process of forming your company. As you will recall, stockholders elect directors, directors elect officers, and resolutions and meetings are required to document these actions.

You will need to complete and sign the following list of documents to elect officers, adopt bylaws, and open a bank account. We have included sample copies of these documents in the Appendix. These forms are available from your public library (where you can also look for books on incorporating):

- Statement of incorporation in lieu of organizational meeting
- First meeting of directors

- ➩ Waiver of notice of meeting
- ➩ Organization meeting minutes form
- ➩ Resolution to open bank account
- ➩ Resolution to adopt bylaws
- ➩ Acceptance of office

HOW TO OBTAIN A TAXPAYER IDENTIFICATION NUMBER

As a sole proprietorship, you generally use your social security number as your taxpayer identification number. You must put this number on each of your individual income tax returns, such as Form 1040 and its schedules. However, every partnership and corporation (including "S" corporations) and certain sole proprietorships must have an employer identification number (EIN) to use as a taxpayer identification number. Sole proprietors must have EINs, if they:

1. Pay wages to one or more employees or
2. Must file any pension or excise tax returns, including those for alcohol, tobacco or firearms.

Application for identification number. To apply for a social security number, you should use Form SS-5. If you are under 18 years of age, you must furnish evidence, along with this form, of age, identity, and U.S. citizenship. If you are 18 or older, you must appear in person with this evidence at a Social Security office.

To apply for an EIN, use form SS-4 (see Appendix One, Start-Your-Own-Business Kit). This form is available from IRS and Social Security Administration offices.

CHAPTER NINE

Protect Your Assets Forever: Your Asset Protection Plan

Chapter Chart

One of the major concerns of most small businesses is lawsuit or liability protection. The reason most people decide to incorporate is to protect their personal assets from litigation by creating a "corporate veil" to cover and protect their family wealth. This chapter will discuss the threat and recommend some alternative solutions.

- ➪ The threat is very serious in America today. Almost 95% of the lawsuits in the world are filed here in the United States with the District of Columbia, Maryland and Virginia ranked the top three jurisdictions in the country for litigation.
- ➪ There are many land mines in the business world. You must be aware of them and have some strategies in place to minimize the risks.
- ➪ Insurance is a start but it will not, most likely, provide you the protection that you will need. Jury awards are just too high today. You must take deliberate, well thought out actions to protect against loss or bankruptcy.
- ➪ In addition to protecting your personal assets, you need also be concerned with the possibile impacts if your corporation suffers a devastating lawsuit. Sure, your personal assets may be protected but what about the corporation's assets? The corporate assets are ultimately the source of your personal income. If they are lost, your family's living income will be affected dramatically.

Lawsuits are one of the most frightening things about being in business. This is an area that is near and dear to our hearts. Having specialized in this area for years, we have watched hundreds upon hundreds of thousands of dollars literally disappear from a family's wealth and estate as a result of a suit. These losses have not only been the result of jury awards, but legal representation can bleed you to death. Even a small garden variety suit, as we mentioned before, could cost $25,000 to $50,000 to fight. A fairly significant misfortune could easily run several hundred thousand dollars. A large newsworthy litigation could bankrupt a multi-millionaire. In the family of one of the authors, legal fees alone ran $300,000 in a single automobile accident case, where the "at fault" driver was drunk and on drugs. You will realize that it doesn't matter whose fault it is—it only matters who has money to go after.

Former Vice President Dan Quayle said during his nomination speech in 1992, "We are experiencing a litigation explosion . . . With 5% of the world's population we have over 90% of the world's lawyers." Estimates vary on the exact number of lawsuits which are filed each year in the United States. Charles Givens in "Wealth Without Risk" reported there were approximately 100,000,000 lawsuits filed each year in the world, with 95% in the U.S. Even the lowest number seen in the U.S. Court Reporter (20,000,000 in 1992) is still a pretty scary 55,000 lawsuits per day. As mentioned in the preceding chapter, many sources state that the *average U.S. small business person will be faced with some type of litigation threat at least five times during the life of the business.* Quayle quantifed the problem further by stating that litigation today is a "$300 billion drain on the economy."

Forbes magazine reported the case of the farmer who hired some Hispanic workers to apply pesticide to his fields. The fertilizer was toxic to animals and the farmer's prize bull died as a result. But that wasn't the end of it. The farmer sued the manufacturer of the pesticide, claiming that the warning instructions printed on the bags should have been printed in Spanish as well as English. He won $13 million, $8 million of which was punitive and thus not insured.

"Defendants, particularly if they are perceived as having money, have begun to find they run the risk of losing lawsuits even if their involvement is minimal," Forbes noted.

Jury Verdict Research, which monitors jury decisions nationwide, notes that the 1990 average award in employment wrongful termination suits hit $311,332. The maximum award was $6.8 million. The research also showed that an employee bringing a wrongful termination suit had an 86% chance of winning!

Litigation and lawsuits in the U.S. have been described recently as "the largest underground wealth re-distribution system in the world." It's up to you to make sure that your business and personal assets and income are protected, and that you have the kind of liability armor that is needed. You must recognize that not only could your assets be taken, but they are the assets you use to generate income, profits and cash to provide for your family. If substantial amounts of assets are lost, you may also lose a substantial amount of annual income; the income you count on to put bread on the table and a roof over your family's head. You can no longer afford to think it will never happen to you. You should take action today to understand to what extent you could be hurt in a lawsuit.

There are many many potential legal land mines in the business world. These explosives get even more dangerous when you consider that most planning assumes honest, upright citizens. Dishonest social parasites increase the threat of unforeseen possibilities. According to Mr. Chris Wyrick, Senior Consultant with Confidential Technologies, Ltd. (St. Louis, MO at 800-413-5694) privacy consultants, the most common threats to your business and wealth are:

- Divorce (yours, your spouse's, your child's, your partner's)
- Real property problem (crack in the pavement, ice, etc)
- Vehicle accident (we think of cars and trucks as lawsuits on wheels)
- Action or error by an employee or contractor
- Equipment malfunction causing injury
- Malpractice
- Wrongful termination
- Sexual harrassment
- Discrimination
- Improper guarantees
- Breach of contract
- Non-performance on a contract

- Copyright, patent infringement
- Inability to repay a loan

Insurance has traditionally been the armor that business people looked toward to protect them—and you should certainly have adequate coverage. But insurance should only be one component in your overall Asset Protection Plan. With jury awards so high, even if you could buy sufficient insurance, you probably couldn't afford it. Additionally, you must look not only at the potential effects on your business, but also how much of your family's assets (home, savings, college fund, retirement plan, etc.) could be lost.

There are several defensive actions you should consider taking.

First, you must be sure that you have all the liability insurance that you need—vehicle, errors and omissions, etc. You should and must read every word in the policies so that you understand and comply with all terms and conditions. We cannot tell you how many times in our practice that we have come across situations where business owners thought they were covered on some matter only to find out too late they were not. A common mistake is that people think a typical umbrella policy is all they need. Many times an umbrella policy will not protect you against business-related actions or losses. You must read the policy to be sure. There are several types of insurance that deserve consideration. The best strategy is to consult with at least three business insurance specialists. Ask them each to give you a proposal. Meet with each insurance consultant and review his or her proposals. Talk with other business people in your area to get their opinions and make your best choice. Nothing is cast in granite. Next year you can change to improve your coverage or bottom line, but do not leave yourself without protection today.

Second, you should be very careful that you have sound business procedures in place to minimize the chances of a business lawsuit. Consider establishing policies and procedures in the areas of personnel, collections, compensation, corporate formalities, advertising, environment and safety. Many times the issue of liability comes down to the paper trail. The more you can show that you took all the right steps, trained your staff and monitored day-to-day performance, the higher the odds will be in your favor.

Third, you should avoid, if at all possible, joint relationships at either a personal or business level. You must be extremely careful when considering a joint relationship in business ventures, with family or non-family members. These joint relationships might result in your business or you being found liable for the actions of your joint partner. At this point, the door might be open to your personal assets. You must be sure that in cases where a partner or partners are required, you have taken necessary precautions with the ownership rights to the business, your personal asset structure and control to ensure your complete safety. Possibilities like the divorce of a partner could result in an angry, bitter spouse controlling a majority interest in your company. The death or incapacitation of a partner could bring your business to its knees and force an avoidable bankruptcy. These situations can be prevented with proper asset protection planning up front.

Fourth, if you are operating as a sole proprietorship, you should seriously and immediately consider reorganizing your business into a legal form that will give you personal liability protection. Forget the reasons your attorney or accountant gives you for not incorporating. The bottom line is that the few hundred extra dollars that it will cost you each year is very well worth the money. You cannot get cheaper liability insurance than this. And besides, there are many tax angles and strategies available that will save you tens or hundreds of times these costs. The most commonly recommended options today are to either incorporate or to form a limited liability company. Either will allow you to make great strides in building your financial fortress. There are also many little known strategies we have developed that can enhance the protection power of corporations or LLCs, one of which will be discussed later in this chapter.

Fifth, when using a liability-limiting business vehicle, like a corporation, you must be sure that you adhere to all the legal formalities necessary to prevent any personal liability exposures. A corporation is no corporation at all unless it walks, talks, and acts like a corporation in every transaction that is performed. Record-keeping formalities are critically important in a small corporation. In the case of a one-person corporation, they are everything.

One of the first things the prosecuting attorney will do when you are being sued as a corporation is attempt to prove that there was no corporation, that the business was you, and the corporation was just a sham. Therefore, the court will be asked to hold out all your personal assets and wealth to pay for the damages. This is known as "piercing the corporate veil." There are several dozen things the courts will look for to decide if you really had a corporation. You can use the list shown on the next few pages as a vehicle to assess the health of your corporation or as a guide to follow when you are operating your corporation. If you follow, at a minimum, these items, you will almost certainly have a solid level of protection in place. IDS of Overland Park, Kansas markets an excellence software product called "Resolution," which totally automates the corporate record-keeping process. They have several different versions that retail from $95 to $295. They can be reached at 1-800-905-5465. IDS has agreed to give purchasers of this book 10% off, so be sure to mention where you read about their product.

CORPORATION PAPERWORK AND FORMALITIES CHECKLIST

1. Have you given proper notice, or used the appropriate waiver of notice, for all meetings of stockholders or Directors?
2. Have you held a first Board of Directors Meeting?
3. Have by-laws for your corporation been adopted by your Board of Directors or Shareholders?
4. Do you have proper and adequate minutes for the first meeting of the Board of Directors of your corporation?
5. Has the Board of your corporation authorized the issuance of the corporation's stock?
6. Has your corporation issued stock yet?
7. Was your corporation properly capitalized?
8. Have you made sure to file all necessary filings in any state in which your corporation is legally doing business?
9. If your corporation is near or over a year old, have you had an annual meeting of your shareholders?
10. Have you been sure to use a corporate resolution of the Board to authorize and document all major corporate acts?

11. Are you sure that you have properly documented all transactions between you and the corporation with resolutions, minutes, etc.?
12. Do you have a resolution documenting the business purposes for any questionable deductions?
13. Have you kept separate books and bank accounts for the corporation and yourself, making sure at all times never to commingle any funds?
14. Are you sure that your tax returns, books of accounts and corporate record books all say the same thing?
15. On every document you've executed, have you done so as a corporate officer by signing with your title?

Sixth, you should consult with a specialist in asset protection. These consultants typically can review your business and financial particulars, identify exposures, design a strategy that will make it virtually impossible for you to lose your assets and wealth, and implement the plan for you. You should be sure to look for a specialist. The average lawyer or accountant will not know all the various risks, strategies and alternative solutions that can be utilized.

Seventh, you should consider the use of multiple corporations. If you are in a particularly risky business like medicine, automotive repair or another dangerous occupation, you can significantly reduce the likelihood of a taking a serious litigation hit by using more than one corporation to hold your business assets. This has been a favorite in the real estate industry for years; however, it will work for every business. The strategy is that you place all the critical assets that you use in your business to generate revenue in one corporation. You then set up and use a second corporation as the operating company. The only assets that need be held in the operating company are cash, some inventory and some receivables. All other business assets reside in a second corporation somewhere. The operating company then leases or rents, for example, the use of these assets. If the operating company is sued, you can literally give the company away. Tomorrow, you form a new operating corporation, re-lease everything to yourself and you are back in business. Not only will this strategy protect these key business assets, but if this is structured correctly, the business will save significantly on state and federal taxes.

We have identified some things that you should consider doing. There are many more alternative strategies that can be implemented to protect your family wealth. A knowledgeable consultant can show you possibilities far beyond anything that you could imagine. To give you some idea of the possibilities, we have included a rather sophisticated technique, easy to utilize today thanks to current technology. The strategy presented has been provided by Lewis Laughlin, president/CEO, Laughlin Associates, in Carson City, Nevada (1-800-648-0966). We have worked with Lewis Laughlin and his team for years to structure and implement asset protection plans for our clients. Typically, we design the plan for our clients and then use the services of Laughlin Associates to complete the process and implementation.

The strategy discussed below takes advantage of two powerful features of corporations:

1. Corporations are considered to be independent legal entities, separate from their owners; and
2. Corporations can be based in any state, regardless of where their owners live.

By taking advantage of these two features, it is possible to make yourself judgment proof and/or legally eliminate state income taxes.

The principles behind this strategy are two companies doing business together. The best liability insurance anybody could have is to be completely poverty stricken and destitute. We also know that if you never make a profit in your home state, you owe no income tax to your home state; that is, if your state income tax is based on net earnings, or profit, or taxable income as most states are. (The exception is an income tax based on gross income.)

1. Incorporate your home state business that you currently derive income from. For purposes of this example, we are going to call your home state corporation, "Red, Inc." That's because your home state operation will have a lot of red ink. It will try and try and try to make a profit, but if it ends up with red ink (losing money) there are no state income taxes to pay. *Note*: Elect a calendar year ending December 31 as the tax year for Red, Inc.

2. Next, set up a Nevada company and make that company a Nevada corporation. For purposes of this example we will call this corporation "Warbucks Nevada, Inc." Warbucks Nevada, Inc. has its corporate base (with an office, bank account, employees, business license and telephone) in tax-free Nevada. *Note*: Elect a fiscal tax year ending June 30 for Warbucks Nevada, Inc.
3. Now Red, Inc. enters the picture. Operating in your home state, Red, Inc. decides it would be a fine idea to buy some products and/or services from Warbucks Nevada, Inc. in Nevada. Remember that Red, Inc. and Warbucks Nevada, Inc. are separate corporations and are therefore separate persons. (A corporation is an artificial person created by law.) Therefore, if Red, Inc. writes a check to Warbucks Nevada, Inc., money is spent by Red, Inc. (your home-state-based person) and money is received by Warbucks Nevada, Inc. (your Nevada-based person). There is an expense in your home state to Red, Inc. and there is income in Nevada to Warbucks Nevada, Inc. There was money earned in Nevada and an expense in your home state. If Red, Inc. spends all its profit, it makes no money for your home state to tax, plus you have an excellent judgment-proofing tool which we'll explain later.

Just what products and services can Warbucks Nevada, Inc. sell to Red, Inc. from Nevada while operating solely in the state of Nevada? What we suggest as the most solid and workable option is that Warbucks Nevada, Inc. simply loan money to Red, Inc. Red, Inc. would simply be buying the use of money from Warbucks Nevada, Inc. When you borrow money, you generally pay interest. Red, Inc. is no exception to that rule. You put money into Warbucks Nevada, Inc. in exchange for stock. Warbucks Nevada, Inc. uses the money that has been invested in it to make money. It does this by loaning that money to Red, Inc. and preferably others as well. The condition of that loan to Red, Inc. is that the money owed is due and payable when Warbucks Nevada, Inc. asks for it (calls the note). The note in this case is a demand promissory note, which means that it's due when Warbucks Nevada, Inc. demands payment.

Also, as any good business does, Warbucks Nevada, Inc. charges Red, Inc., your home-state operation, interest on the money that it has loaned to Red, Inc. Remember that Warbucks Nevada, Inc. is located in and operating from Nevada. Nevada has no usury laws, so Warbucks Nevada, Inc. charges Red, Inc. whatever interest rate Warbucks Nevada, Inc. thinks is fair. In our example we'll say the rate is 18%. The interest is due each month or year. The interest may even be compounded monthly. This will get Red, Inc. even further in debt to Warbucks Nevada, Inc., which can be very beneficial as you'll see later.

To summarize so far, Red, Inc. borrows money from Warbucks Nevada, Inc. at 18% interest per year with the principal balance due upon demand (when Warbucks Nevada, Inc. calls the note). The money owed to Warbucks Nevada, Inc. is evidenced by a demand promissory note signed and executed by Red, Inc. (the debtor) at the Nevada offices of Warbucks Nevada, Inc. This shows that the money is borrowed in Nevada and, if worded correctly, that the note is governed by the laws of Nevada. How much does Red, Inc. borrow from Warbucks Nevada, Inc.? Well, at 18% simple interest (used only for example because with no usury laws in Nevada, Warbucks could charge more) if Red, Inc. borrowed $100,000, this would mean a business interest expense to Red, Inc. in your home state of at least $18,000 in one year; or the interest could be compounded monthly.

Depending upon the amount of money borrowed and the interest rate that the two companies (which you own) agree upon, the interest expense to Red, Inc. in your home state could be as high or as low as you decide. *Note*: This strategy works just as well if you sold products (and services) to Red, Inc. instead of lending it money. Warbucks Nevada, Inc. sells the products and services to Red, Inc. and takes back a promissory note due and payable when Warbucks Nevada, Inc. calls it. Interest on that note is due monthly (maybe with interest compounded monthly) or yearly. That interest is still an expense to Red, Inc. and the result can be the same: no profit for Red, Inc. in your home state. The principal amount of the note may also be deductible to Red, Inc.

Judgment Proof

The stage is already set. All that remains are a few simple steps to make your business operation judgment proof. Warbucks Nevada, Inc. is based in Nevada and it maintains a low profile. It's merely financing a few things here and there for profit. Its main client is Red, Inc., which you own. Warbucks Nevada, Inc.'s chances of getting sued are one in a million.

The idea is to make Red, Inc. judgment proof, to turn Red, Inc. into a turnip that no one can bleed and at the same time make sure it has the money, equipment, fixtures, land, buildings, etc., to conduct your business.

Debt. Red, Inc. borrows money from Warbucks Nevada, Inc. every time it gets a chance. It probably even finances part of its interest payments due to Warbucks Nevada, Inc. because it can't quite make them all in cash. Therefore, each month or year the debt keeps increasing. It would not be hard to establish a debt so large to Warbucks Nevada, Inc. that it eclipses the value of all the assets of Red, Inc.

Let's say Red, Inc. has assets totaling $250,000 which you want to protect. Red, Inc. borrows and borrows from Warbucks Nevada, Inc., getting deeper and deeper in debt. Finally, it's at least $250,000 or more in debt. The debt figure is limited only by the principal amount Warbucks Nevada, Inc. and Red, Inc. agree upon and the corresponding interest rate.

Security agreement. Warbucks Nevada, Inc. is going to make sure they get paid or else. So Warbucks Nevada, Inc. will want some collateral on the loan to Red, Inc. Warbucks Nevada, Inc. and Red, Inc. enter into a "security agreement." This is a common, powerful tool that is used to secure certain assets as collateral on a loan. With this security agreement they agree that the assets, receivables, inventory, and everything belonging to Red, Inc. are collateral for that loan. On any equity in real property Red, Inc. would issue a trust deed (mortgage) to Warbucks Nevada, Inc.

Financing statement. As notice to the world that these assets are collateral for a debt owed to Warbucks Nevada, Inc. in Nevada, Warbucks Nevada, Inc. will record what is called a "UCC-1" financing statement with the Secretary of State's office in Nevada and with the Secretary of State's office and appropriate county recorders in your home state. This UCC-1 form states that these assets are collateral for a note that is owed. It gives notice to the world that these assets are encumbered and that no one can touch these assets until the debt owed to Warbucks Nevada, Inc. is paid. *Note*: UCC-1 filings and the security agreement that perfects a security interest in the assets of Red, Inc. come before everything else (except some tax claims). In other words Warbucks Nevada, Inc. is in a first position on all of the assets that Red, Inc. owns and those assets can't be touched until Warbucks Nevada, Inc. is paid.

Lawsuit. What happens if Red, Inc. gets sued? When the lawyer and the person suing Red, Inc. check out what it has that they can take, they get a very rude awakening. They search to see what Red, Inc. is worth. That includes looking for any real property the corporation owns along with any debt against it and any UCC-1 filings encumbering the assets Red, Inc. may own. They find a big debt—they find all of the assets of Red, Inc. are encumbered. Red, Inc. is worthless.

That's probably the end of the lawsuit against Red, Inc. On the other hand, let's say the person suing you files the lawsuit. He even gets a judgment. Now what happens?

Remember Warbucks Nevada, Inc. is owed money by Red, Inc. as evidenced by a promissory note due on demand. When Warbucks Nevada, Inc. calls the note, Red, Inc. has to pay. Warbucks Nevada, Inc. decides it is time to get paid. They call the note. Red, Inc. can't pay such a large debt. Warbucks Nevada, Inc. has no recourse except to execute on its security interests. In other words Warbucks Nevada, Inc. takes the assets of Red, Inc. to satisfy the debt.

Large Debt

What happened? That's the same question the attorney who sued you is asking. He's got a judgment against Red, Inc. and Red, Inc. has nothing to execute that judgment on. In fact, you could even call that attorney and tell him, "I'll just give you the whole corporation, come on down and get it." Because even though Warbucks Nevada, Inc. has taken the assets of Red, Inc., the debt that Red, Inc. owed to Warbucks Nevada, Inc. may have been so large that Red, Inc. still owes money to Warbucks Nevada, Inc. That being the case, the only thing a person suing the company would gain is a large debt owed to Warbucks Nevada, Inc. which you own.

Let's review the exact sequence of steps again.

1. Red, Inc. owes Warbucks Nevada, Inc. money.
2. The money Red, Inc. owes Warbucks Nevada, Inc. is evidenced by a promissory note due when Warbucks Nevada, Inc. says it's due.
3. As security or collateral on that note Warbucks Nevada, Inc. and Red, Inc. have agreed that the assets of Red, Inc. will be collateral and security for the note.
4. As notice to the world and evidence of the fact that these assets are collateral on the loan, a UCC-1 filing is done in Nevada and in your home state, and a trust deed is executed on any real property and filed in the county in which the property is located.
5. Warbucks Nevada, Inc. is in a first position on the assets of Red, Inc. and no one suing Red, Inc. can touch those assets until the debt to Warbucks Nevada, Inc. (that you own) is paid.
6. You are doing business "judgment proof," because even if there is a judgment against Red, Inc., there is nothing to take.

The choice is yours. You can take action, bulletproof your company, your wealth and your future, or you can stand by and hope that it will never happen to you. A well-designed plan can be gradually phased in over time. Everything does not have to be done at one time unless, for some reason, you are in a precarious position. The sooner you put things in place, the more effective they will be. There are many legal statutes concerning assets, their restructure and transfer, which could render your plans useless. Plans made within two years prior to a suit being filed are particularly vulnerable.

You can rationalize that you will be careful, that you would never act illegally or without the highest level of honesty. Nevertheless, a business person can unknowingly and unintentionally get into trouble. Our recommendation is to protect yourself.

CHAPTER TEN

The Money Trail

"If you think you know the value of money, try and borrow some."

BENJAMIN FRANKLIN

Chapter Chart

How will you finance your life in business? This chapter shows you where to look for start-up capital and how to play the banking game and come out on top.

- Many people start with the money they can scrape together from their own savings and money from their friends and family.
- Government agencies, venture capitalists and finance companies each have something to offer the new business owner in search of capital.
- Not all banks are created equal. Some are truly helpful while some are like sharks in the water. You can learn to tell the difference.

INTRODUCTION

Your business cannot begin without money. You need to secure a location, hire employees, stock your shelves and advertise—all before your first customer walks in the door. Unless you are sitting on a pile of money, you will have to find the funds you need to start your business.

While it's true that banks are a significant source of loaned money, they are not the only or the most desirable source available. You also can obtain money from venture capitalists, finance companies, government agencies, friends and relatives—often on more favorable terms than a bank can offer. A recent survey from *Inc.* magazine found that 78.5% of seed capital comes from savings.

Piggy Bank Financing

Countless businesses have been started with the owner cleaning out his or her savings account and adding small contributions from relatives, friends and neighbors who are willing to make a loan on the merits of their relationship. If you can generate enough money to get off the ground this way, by all means do so. It's the most accessible type of financing around, and it has the added benefit of making your friends and family feel good about being able to help you.

The major problem with this kind of financing is that you usually cannot generate an ample supply of money—you may have to live and work at near-starvation levels to make ends meet. Furthermore, you are temporarily living off your friends' goodwill and you may feel considerable pressure to pay back your debts faster than you can afford to.

Take the case of Kathy Casadei, owner of the Compleat Jeweler in Santa Fe, New Mexico. Kathy used piggy bank financing to open her business. A year ago she scoured the pockets of relatives and friends to finance the gala opening of her pricey jewelry store. Though business has been good, Kathy still has a long way to go before she can settle her debts. Because Kathy is so close to her creditors, she wants to pay them back now. "I know my Aunt Mary would buy a new car if she had her $3,000 back," she says. "Sometimes I feel like handing it over no matter what it does to my cash flow."

Some entrepreneurs in Kathy's position have solved the problem by taking out a bank loan a year or so into operation and using the money to pay back initial investors. A banker is more likely to lend you money once you have a history of sales and sound management.

Government Funding

Governmental agencies can often prove a reliable and accessible source of funding. At the top of the list is the Small Business Administration (SBA) which can provide loans at moderate interest rates or can guarantee loans made by banks. In a loan guarantee, the SBA promises to pay the bank in case you default on the loan.

Though SBA loans and guarantees are becoming more scarce in these days of social program spending cuts, it pays to check out this potential source of income. The SBA still lends millions of dollars every year. You can obtain a list of SBA offices around the country by writing to the SBA, Office of Public Information, Room 100, 1441 L Street, N.W., Washington, D.C. 20416.

State, county and community agencies sometimes offer loans to small businesses at attractive rates. These loans are often contingent on the location or type of business being started. In our community, businesses wishing to locate in a specific three-block area qualify for attractive start-up loans because the county is trying to revitalize commerce there. While qualifications for these loans vary widely, a little legwork on your part can land you a hefty chunk of money with few strings attached.

FINANCE COMPANIES

Finance companies advance money to less mature businesses than do commercial banks. New business owners find that finance companies are a last resort for funding. They determine loan eligibility on assets rather than credit histories and income projections.

While borrowing money against your assets can be an advantage in some situations, it is also very risky. You may lose everything if your business is not successful.

Finance company money is also more expensive than bank money. The reason is simple: The company knows you can't get the loan elsewhere, and it will charge you whatever interest rate it wants.

Some business advisers recommend avoiding finance companies entirely because of their cutthroat tactics. This policy is a little extreme. If you find you need to work with a finance company, proceed with extreme caution. The specifics differ from company to company, so be sure you and your lawyer carefully check all the terms of the agreement before you sign anything.

VENTURE CAPITALISTS

Venture capitalists are private investors who provide seed money to new businesses with exceptional growth potential. Investment firms, large industrial companies, insurance companies, trust funds and wealthy individuals are potential sources of venture capital.

Venture capitalists differ from banks in that they seek to protect their investment by asking for a degree of control over the business. They may want input into managerial decisions. Or they may want complete control of the company if certain financial objectives are not met by a certain date. A useful rule of thumb is that the more capital an investor risks on your business, the larger share of control he or she will expect in return.

Many venture capitalists are highly experienced in new business management, having been part of many ventures in a relatively short span of time. Most business owners who use venture capital quickly recognize their investors as a resource for a wide range of financial and managerial information. Not only do these owners obtain capital, but they get easy access to expert advice whenever they need it.

Attracting Venture Capital

For venture capitalists to seriously consider investing in your firm, they must be convinced that their money will see a phenomenal rate of return. Phenomenal, in this case, translates to the neighborhood of 35 to 50% per year. You have to be willing to work hard to make the profits that allow you to pay venture capitalists that kind of return. If you have the energy, they have the money to back you!

A national directory of venture capitalists, with information about each, is available from the National Venture Capital Association, 1655 North Fort Myer Drive, Suite 700, Arlington, Virginia 22209. You might also find sources of venture capital in business magazines such as *Venture* and *Inc.*, or in your local business publication.

THE BANKING GAME

Banks are definitely the old standby in the world of business financing. The best among them deserve their reputation as community builders, helping businesses and individuals prosper through sound money management. Unfortunately, some banks think that they are doing you a favor by providing services.

Since your investor is going to be in your life a long time, it pays to know what kind of institution or individual you are dealing with. Familiarize yourself with a number of banks in your area to get a feel for whether they operate with concern for their customers and the larger community or for profit alone.

Killer Banks

Killer banks are profit pirates. They lend freely when interest rates are low and call back their loans—in full—as soon as interest rates rise. Then they lend the money out again at a higher rate of interest.

One experience with a killer bank can be a blow to a small business owner. To identify killer banks, consult with your lawyer, accountant or banking insider who knows the reputations of banks in your community.

Loan Officers

The other way to get a picture of your bank's orientation is to sit down with one or more of its loan officers and discuss your plans. Are the loan officers patient and friendly? Are they knowledgeable about the local business climate? Have they funded businesses of your size before? Are they willing to be frank about whether they think your business will succeed?

Try asking your loan officer for advice about your financing options. If he or she is responsive and genuinely interested in helping you, you have probably found a good place to do your banking.

Think of the loan officer as the first gate-keeper between you and the piles of money in the vault. He or she can veto your application right away or send it to the committees that give the final approval.

However, you want a loan officer who will send your application to the committee only if he or she is convinced it will be approved. In the world of banking, having a credit application turned down can result in a "black mark" on your credit report. You definitely want to avoid it at all costs. An astute loan officer can save you from this fate by advising you not to apply if your chances aren't very good.

Loan Lessons

Once you've found a place to borrow money and a loan officer you can work with, you're ready for the application process itself.

There are several things you should keep in mind as you journey down the money trail.

1. Ask for more than you need. If you need $40,000, ask for $50,000. Cover yourself. You don't want to run out of money because the market throws you a curve ball.
2. Don't exaggerate. Painting a fantastic portrait of your business potential will backfire. Your banker will quickly show you to the door. If you've followed the suggestions in Chapter Three, you won't need to exaggerate because you will have a solid, well-thought-out plan that is sure to impress lenders. With your business plan, you can maintain unflagging confidence, yet remain realistic about possible pitfalls.

   Also, be realistic about your own credit history. It's futile to try to hide blots on your credit record; your banker will find them anyway. Be prepared to give good reasons for any difficulties you've had, and show how you've learned from the experience.
3. Be realistic about repayment. Don't agree to a repayment schedule that is out of line with your potential cash flow. Try to keep payments as low as possible or have them start out low and gradually increase over a few years. Nothing irks a banker or ruins a credit record faster than late or missed payments on a loan.
4. Consider your banker's advice. If your loan officer has suggestions that make your plan more appealing to the loan committee, consider them seriously. This person has been through the process countless times. You can benefit from his or her experience only if you are willing to listen.
5. Avoid giving a personal guarantee. Most banks will want you to give a personal endorsement on a loan. They may even want your spouse to sign. This is too risky. If anything goes wrong, you could lose a whole lot more than your business.

6. Don't let rejection get you down. Everyone is rejected at some point in business. Give yourself the chance to get mad, sad or worried, then pick up and go on.

A FINAL WORD

A start-up business needs money like a seedling needs water. Your job as a beginning entrepreneur is to find the right amount of money at the right price under the right terms. With careful preparation and a proceed-with-caution approach, you can get what you and your business need to prosper. There are investors waiting for your call! A detailed list of funding sources can be found in Appendix Two, Recommended Resources.

Sources of Funding for Your Business—Compare Your Options

PRIVATE SOURCES

—Your money
—Relatives, friends and neighbors

Positives	Negatives
—Easier to access —Can make family and friends glad to assist	—Added stress element to pay back —May undercapitalize

GOVERNMENT FUNDING

—Small Business Administration
—Federal, state, county and community agency programs

Positives	Negatives
—Attractive interest rates	—Be prepared to answer potentially difficult questions for audit purposes; e.g.: hiring practices and financial operations —May require a long and difficult application process

FINANCE COMPANIES

Positives	Negatives
—Easier to access than bank money	—Higher interest —Cutthroat tactics employed by some finance companies

VENTURE CAPITALISTS

Positives	Negatives
—Fair interest rates —Good seed money source —Usually a good source of experienced management	—Often want some control of the business

BANKS

Positives	Negatives
—Sound financial resource and management experience —Reasonable rates	—Avoid killer banks —Avoid killer loans

CHAPTER ELEVEN

Location Is Everything

"A foolish man built his house upon the sand."
BOOK OF MATTHEW

Chapter Chart

Location is a crucial factor in your success equation. This chapter outlines the challenges you face when choosing a location that's right for your business.

- Your best location bargain may be your own home! Learn which kinds of businesses work well at home and which do not.
- For retail shops and restaurants, the three most important survival factors are location, location and location—in that order. Knowing how to pick the best spot for your business is a survival skill you must learn.
- If you can't afford your ideal location, you can still make a go of it. Learn how to beat the location game through effective advertising and promotion.

INTRODUCTION

As you get closer to opening your business, you need to think about a very important question: Where are you going to put it? Although this seems ridiculously fundamental, many would-be business owners often overlook it and regret it later.

For some types of businesses, such as consulting firms, mail-order businesses or delivery services, location is important but not crucial. For others, including retail shops and restaurants, location is so important that it may be the deciding factor in whether the business survives.

A Penny Saved

One of your major priorities as a new business owner is to reduce costs wherever you can. In addition to labor costs, you're going to have four major expenses:

1. Rent
2. Equipment
3. Inventory
4. Promotion

The more you can save on rent and equipment the more you'll have for inventory and promotion: two things important to your survival in the first couple of years.

Before you spend a lot of money on plush office space, first-class furnishings and state-of-the-art equipment, consider that there may be a less expensive way. A study by the Suffolk University Business School found that 92% of new businesses could have started with lower expenses for rent, equipment and supplies with no drop in sales and a healthy jump in profits.

You don't make money by simply throwing money around. You make money by judiciously investing it when and where it's needed. Cut corners where you can.

There's No Place Like Home

One start-up location is right underfoot. If you start your business in your home, you avoid paying extra rent and being locked into a lease before you know how much money you can make.

You also save on taxes. Part of your rent, utilities and other bills are legitimate business expenses. If you use 25% of your home for your business, for example, you can claim 25% of your home expenses (rent, utilities, etc.) as tax deductions. Just be sure you can document your use of that portion of your home for the business only.

According to James Wills, a CPA of Fredericksburg, VA, these are the guidelines for home office deductions:

1. The office portion must be used exclusively and on a regular basis as your principal place of business.
2. The deduction is limited to the net income from the home office business before deducting home office expenses. Any excess deductions can be carried forward and used in later years.
3. If you own your home, depreciation can be taken on the proportion of your home that is used for your business.
4. If you rent your home, you can take a percentage of the rent.

Finally, you save money and time every day because you don't have to commute. This is especially important in urban areas where traffic, exorbitant parking fees, and late trains are a fact of life.

> *"You may have to start out on the kitchen table or in a corner of the living room. Millions have started the same way and that's okay—for a while. To make the most out of working at home, though, you'll need to begin planning ways to make your working space more comfortable, efficient, and permanent."*
>
> LYNIE ARDEN, *THE WORK AT HOME SOURCEBOOK*

TEN BEST BUSINESSES TO START AT HOME

- Courier and Messenger Services
- Catering and Party Planning
- Child and Elderly Day Care
- Carpentry Services
- Cleaning and Maintenance Services
- Mail-Order Retailing
- Visiting Nurse Services
- Dating Services
- Aerobics and Exercise Instruction
- Tour Guide Services

Before you set up a business at home, find out about local zoning ordinances. If you live in a rural area, chances are you will encounter few regulations. But in populated areas, laws may prohibit certain kinds of businesses in residential neighborhoods to protect them from disruptive noise, traffic, odors or other nuisances.

Working at home presents some unique problems. The border between work and your personal life may get fuzzy. You may find yourself sneaking away to deal with family matters, personal phone calls or a suddenly important snack at great cost to your efficiency.

There may be a question of space. If you work in the midst of your living area, the time you spend setting up and breaking down operations every day could take away from your work.

Also, having your home double as an office might make you feel less professional. It can make your position as a newcomer more apparent and might give your customers the feeling that they are dealing with a fly-by-night operation.

Some of these problems are easily remedied. For about $15 per month, you can hire a prestigious mail drop service and have a swanky address. For about $50 to $75 per month you can rent office space for an hour or two—for meetings with key customers.

ONWARD AND UPWARD

There will come a time, perhaps sooner than you think, when your business will outgrow your home. Inexpensive yet adequate office space may be difficult but not impossible to find. Commercial real estate agents usually avoid budget properties—they need to close pricier deals to make higher commissions. To find bargains you have to look for them, but the time spent searching can pay for itself in the long run.

Office basements can be bargains. Many businesses ready for expansion start by splitting their operations. They rent presentable office space for sales purposes and house the rest of their operations in the basement.

Older homes can be made into inexpensive office space. Before you sign the lease, however, make sure that local zoning laws allow business to be conducted in the area. Don't get stuck with unusable space!

It pays to be innovative. Spaces such as boarded-up gas stations, diners, and factories often can be renovated at low cost. Sometimes the building's owner will finance the work to attract tenants.

WHERE THE CUSTOMERS ARE

Business experts rarely agree on anything. One thing they all believe, however, is that the three most important factors in the survival of a retail business are **location, location** and **location**—in that order.

Cheap is out, expensive is in if you're planning a retail start-up. Finding your prime location takes some research. Let's take a look at the factors to consider as you shop for your prospective site.

Greener Pastures

The first thing to consider is whether to locate your business in your home town or seek greener pastures. While personal preference should be a big factor in your decision, you also should consider whether your target area can support the kind of business you'd like to start.

Ray's Bait and Tackle Shop in his home town of Nags Head, North Carolina, is located in the middle of prime fishing territory. But if Ray were from the Arizona desert, he might have had to move to find the client base necessary to support his business.

Sometimes it's best not to leave your home turf. Contacts, especially in the financial community, are important. In your home town you undoubtedly have creditors who know you and a network of people who will help you get going. Your friends are your best first customers. Ask each friend to tell 12 people what a great service or product you provide.

Demographics

Demographics is Madison Avenue's term for finding out what the people in a certain region are like. As you know from your marketing study in Chapter Two, you must know what the people in your target area need and want, how much money they make, whether they have kids, and so on. This information helps you judge whether they will be interested in your product or service and whether they can afford it.

In addition to getting the current picture of the people in your target area, you should also consider what the future will bring. Will certain kinds of people be moving in or out in the next few years? What kinds of products or services will they need or want?

Traffic Patterns

> *"Subconsciously consider your customers as stupid and lazy. By lazy, assume they will not lift a finger to go out of their way to buy your product or service. By stupid, presume the customer is unable to read a map. The objective is to place the business in a location so obvious it cannot be overlooked."*
>
> JAMES HALLORAN, *THE ENTREPRENEUR'S GUIDE TO STARTING A BUSINESS*

You can have a terrific idea, adequate financing, and a beautiful setup, and still fail. Why? Because you are located too far out of the way. You have to locate your business where customers will find you.

One way to find good locations for your business is to take a look around your target community. If you're **in** the city, you'll probably want to follow mass transit and walking routes. In the suburbs, you'll want to check out main thoroughfares and commuter routes.

Which routes seem reasonably busy? Are there landmarks that people pass frequently? Are there major attractions such as beaches, sports stadiums or parks? Wherever people already go is a good spot to do business.

Whether in the city or suburbs, you need to pay attention to parking. Never assume your customers will drive in circles looking for a parking spot just for the privilege of patronizing your store. Chances are they'll find another store that offers hassle-free parking.

Competition

It's vitally important to be aware of your competitors at all times. If you don't have a solid edge on them in terms of price, quality or customer service—you'll want them to be well out of your way. For example, if you set up your hamburger stand between McDonald's and Burger King, you're asking for trouble. Your neighbors will surely outadvertise or under-price you until you're starved out.

Even though Ray Kroc, founder of McDonald's, believes "saturation is for sponges," you ought to pay attention to this critical aspect of locating your business. Not all of us start out with an idea as irresistible as the one that propelled Kroc to fame and fortune!

Also, the number of people doing a particular business in an area is important to your success. Suppose your area contains seven dry cleaning establishments, each of which is breaking even. Business moguls would say the dry cleaning market in your area is saturated and unable to support further business. If you're hooked on the idea of being a dry cleaner, you'd do well to look elsewhere for a home for your firm.

The Company You Keep

Not all of your neighbors are your competitors. Some neighbors may have a beneficial effect on your business. Locating near a popular department store, for example, practically guarantees a large volume of traffic in the vicinity of your store. Many a shopping mall has been built around one or two major department stores whose large clientele then becomes available to the smaller surrounding stores.

Milo Barrari put his Casa di Roma pizza shop next to the local movie house. People coming to see a movie could also enjoy a solid meal and a nice evening out.

Certain combinations of businesses can maximize each other's profits.

The maxim "You are judged by the company you keep" couldn't be more true in the retail business. The environment in which you work sends a strong message to your customers about the quality and price of your products.

Hannah's Hosiery is a case in point. An upscale intimate apparel store, Hannah's is located in a refurbished turn-of-the-century train station in Washington, D.C. The station's ambience projects an image of quality—an image that enhances the businesses within.

Of course, businesses wishing to sell on the budget end of the spectrum wouldn't want to locate in Hannah's mall. Such businesses couldn't afford the overhead. Also, customers who buy budget products wouldn't shop in a pricey mall. These customers would prefer stores on the local highway strip where goods are priced and packaged to appeal to their sense of practicality, as well as to their pocketbook.

Off The Beaten Path

Even if you find the perfect spot for your business, you may not be able to afford it. You may have to begin in a less-than-ideal location, but that is an obstacle that can be overcome.

One successful alternative to a high-priced location is to create a powerful, aggressive and expert promotional campaign. Of course, this is costly, but you must let people know where you are. Hire a good advertising or public relations firm. Chapter Thirteen offers an excellent introduction to the world of promotion and explains how you can get the most out of your advertising dollars.

But even with the best promotion, you'll still need patience. It can take weeks, perhaps years, to build the reputation that brings customers to your door. Be prepared to wait.

"Learn to say no when a site doesn't meet your criteria. You just have to keep turning over rocks to find the worms. There are too many problems with low volume locations and too many opportunities for superstars, for you to take chances . . ."

Philip Holland, *The Entrepreneur's Guide*

Where To Get Help

When choosing your business location, you may have to search for what seems like a long time. A year or more is not unusual. You may want to consider hiring consultants that specialize in determining which locations suit your retail needs. It's best to bring in consultants when you've narrowed down your choices to about two or three, so you don't pay for work you could do yourself.

Sources

Other places to go for help are your local Chamber of Commerce and your local office of the Small Business Administration. These agencies specialize in helping businesses find good locations or professional assistance for locating a business.

Possible Locations to Consider for Your Business

Home

—Positives

—Avoids extra rent payment
—Possible tax write-off
—Saves commuting expense

—Negatives

—Possible conflict with neighborhood zoning laws or restrictive covenants
—Space may be limited
—Easier to be distracted
—Less professional image

Bargain Offices

—Office basements
—Small sales offices
—Older homes
—Boarded-up commercial property

Retail Offices

—Is prime location needed?
—Is home town best location?
—Consider your target area: traffic patterns, customer parking, saturated market?

CHAPTER TWELVE

Setting Up Shop

"A miser is a person who lives within his income. He is also called a magician."
ROBERT FROST

Chapter Chart

You've found your dream location. Now what? This chapter shows you how savvy business owners negotiate with landlords, get needed renovations, find furniture and equipment and begin operations.

- No lease is final until you sign it. Learn how to negotiate with your landlord to get the best rent, security deposit and renewal terms for your business.
- Renovations are often important considerations when you sign on to a site. Know whether your landlord will finance renovations—before you sign.
- New business owners frequently overspend on furniture and equipment, which can cause a cash flow crisis later on. Find out how to get furniture and equipment at rock-bottom prices.
- Well before you open your doors, you are involved in many financial transactions. Learn how to keep tabs on the money rushing in and out of your business's bank account, so you always know how much cash you have.

Setting up shop is more than putting a sign in the window and waiting for the customers to walk in. It also means negotiating favorable leases, getting needed renovations, and finding bargains in furniture and equipment. It means hiring employees and finding suppliers to provide you with merchandise and supplies. It means learning how to keep careful financial records of every business transaction you make.

WORKING WITH LANDLORDS

Unless you're going to work out of your home, one of the first steps in setting up shop is signing a lease on commercial office or retail space. The commercial lease is often lengthy and complicated, and it has an enduring impact on your bottom line. To protect your profits, you need to be familiar with and understand its terms and clauses.

All leases state a basic rent charge (per square foot of floor space per year), a security deposit to cover damages to the property during your occupancy, and a duration requirement, usually three to five years but often longer. Most leases describe your renewal options.

> *"Renting is very elastic in terms of supply and demand. If the landlord is having trouble securing leases, or if your particular business would be an asset to his existing tenant mix, much of the lease can be negotiated. Too many inexperienced entrepreneurs fall victim to signing the lease as offered."*
>
> JAMES HALLORAN,
> *ENTREPRENEUR'S GUIDE TO STARTING A SUCCESSFUL BUSINESS*

After these basics, leases can be specific about such things as the hours the business may operate, the kinds of merchandise that may be sold, and the kinds of insurance the tenant must carry.

Since the specifics vary from lease to lease and often appear innocent enough when written in strange and difficult language (legalese), it's best to show any lease you want to sign to a lawyer *before* you sign.

One more thing: Never be afraid to negotiate. Your landlord probably has an urgent need to get a tenant on the property.

Advertising and showing the property to potential renters is time consuming and expensive. Moreover, the landlord must pay the mortgage out-of-pocket when the property isn't generating rental income. You can use these facts to your advantage when negotiating options on your lease.

Let's look at the major components of the lease and discuss how you can turn each into an advantage.

Rent

Sales are never so slow as when you first set up shop. You need to keep cash on hand to see you through these first lean months. One way to keep rent payments from gobbling up your limited cash reserves is to bargain for deferred rent.

In a deferred rent arrangement, you pay a lower rent during the first few months of the lease. In later months, when you can better afford it, you agree to pay a correspondingly higher rent. The net result is that you pay the same total amount of rent as you would in a regular rent arrangement, but payments are adjusted to make it easier for you.

How much can you negotiate on rent? It depends on the desperation level of your landlord. Landlords need cash like everybody else, and sometimes they face a cash crisis. If you're willing to risk losing the site, you could push the issue to see how much your landlord will give in. We've known of truly desperate landlords giving up to six months free rent—quite a savings for a little bargaining!

Mitch Taylor, of Reno Contractors Inc., negotiated a deferred rent arrangement with his landlord. For the first 10 months of his lease, he paid \$300 less per month than the regular \$800 rent. For the following 10 months, he paid the regular figure. But during the 10 months after that, he paid back the extra \$300 per month—making his monthly rent \$1,100 per month. Therefore, he paid the higher rent at a time when he could better afford it—when his business was well established.

Security Deposits

Another item that can be negotiated to save you money when you're starting out is the security deposit. Landlords routinely ask for three to six months' rent for security deposits. With terms like these, you can be priced out of an otherwise affordable location.

One way around the security deposit problem is to spread out the payment over several months or to make it payable at a later time. Another way is to pledge personal collateral, such as your car or home equity, for an amount equal to the deposit. A third way is to find someone to act as a guarantor, whose liability is limited to the amount of the deposit.

Sally Martin of Fakon Cleaners combined the first and third options when trying to come up with her $1,500 security deposit. She asked her mother-in-law to assume liability for the amount for 10 months. Then, five months into operation, she began paying the deposit in monthly installments of $300 until it was paid. Sally gained valuable time in her battle to save start-up cash.

Duration and Renewal

A good location is hard to find, so you should keep yours as long as you can. First, it's bad business to move. Customers don't like searching for your new location.

Second, it's expensive to move, with utility hookups, mover's fees, and time taken from serving customers. Add the cost of changing stationery, invoices and advertisements that have your old address on them, and you've got a hefty sum.

The longer you keep your lease, the longer your rent remains constant. Though your landlord will want cost-of-living increases every year or so, these are nothing compared with the way your rent would jump if you signed a new lease elsewhere.

While three to five years is standard for commercial leases, longer is certainly negotiable. You'll save money and your landlord will be pleased at the thought of avoiding vacancies.

Renovations

Getting the renovations you need to begin operations in an optimal environment is an important step in setting up shop. Your job in this process is to make a list of the work that needs to be done and get reliable estimates on the cost of the work. Then you will be ready to negotiate with your landlord to finance the renovations for you.

The best time to bring up the subject of renovations is after you've shown that you are seriously interested in the property, but before you've signed the lease. Until you sign you have bargaining power. After the deal is closed, your landlord has the upper hand, and any verbal promises not put into writing in the lease are unenforceable.

If you've asked for reasonable renovations and negotiated fairly with your landlord, you should get what you want without too much trouble. In case you run across an inflexible landlord, think carefully about whether you want this person in your life for several years. If the landlord is inflexible now, how will he or she be over the next few years?

TIPS ON RENOVATIONS AND YOUR LANDLORD

- Most seasoned landlords expect to make renovations for commercial tenants.
- It's his or her property. Renovation increases its value, which means a better return when it's rented or sold later on.
- Your landlord may be able to finance renovations by borrowing against the equity in the property.
- Avoid assuming the burden of financing renovations. Your new business needs to preserve your borrowing power—not renovate someone else's property.
- Watch out for back-door financing. Some landlords may try to overcharge you and make a profit on work you've requested!

Legalese

Beware of legalese that may contain unfair terms and clauses. The most common of these is the percentage rent clause, which entitles your landlord to a percentage of your profits if you exceed a certain sales volume during the term of the lease.

Say, for example, your lease has a percentage rent clause at the $100,000 mark. If you break $100,000 in sales your first year, you will have to pay a percentage of your yearly profits in addition to your regular monthly rent.

Protect yourself from legalese and other unwelcome surprises. Have a lawyer discuss every aspect of your lease with you. Don't skimp on lawyer's fees—they may save you money later on.

Furniture And Equipment

One of the most understandable mistakes new business owners make occurs when they begin decorating their office or retail space. Ordinarily prudent people often spend too much as they eye choice furnishings and imagine meetings conducted at mahogany and leather conference suites.

Cut corners where you can. Scour classified ads, auction notices and used furniture stores for bargains on the items you need. While it's easy to use a credit card and take home an office suite, doing so can cause trouble later.

One money-saver for new businesses is furniture rental. Renting is the equivalent of getting a loan, because you get the goods up front but you don't have to pay for them all at once. Over the long term renting is expensive, but for the first few months renting can help you avoid the lean look.

Some businesses find good bargains by snapping up furniture from franchises. To keep an up-to-date image, chains remodel often. The result is a surplus of moderately worn furniture and equipment, available for resale to start-ups. Keep an eye on the classified and business sections of your newspaper for information on bargains like these.

Many start-ups fail because they overspend on rent and equipment. Don't fall victim to this deadly business habit. Later, as profits mount and tax shelters become important, you'll have plenty of time for mahogany and leather.

Keeping The Books

One of the main chores in any business is bookkeeping. When you keep the books, you are maintaining a careful record of your daily cash flow. All money coming in—every check arriving by mail, every dollar put in the cash register—must be carefully noted. On the other end, every dollar going out—for payroll, supplies and overhead—must also be recorded. And if you're in retail, you must keep an accurate record of all inventory, which is really just cash in another form.

As you might guess, bookkeeping can be complicated. Growing businesses perform a hundred or more transactions every day. Nevertheless, you can learn to keep your books in a way that will satisfy the most exacting accountant.

You should be careful never to commingle personal and business funds, especially with corporations, partnerships, or LLCs. In addition to having tax consequences, doing so could leave you open to personal liability.

It's not difficult, but it does take patience and a fondness for detail work. If you're the kind of person who hates hunching over an adding machine getting all of your columns to add up right, you may want to delegate your bookkeeping tasks to someone else. Find an accountant to take care of the books.

An accountant could be invaluable in performing other functions in addition to bookkeeping:

1. To help set up an accounting system for you.
2. To assist you in accounting and financial decisions.
3. To prepare financial statements.
4. To guide you in tax matters.
5. To prepare business and personal tax returns.

There are several key terms you should know—single-entry bookkeeping, double-entry bookkeeping, journal and ledger.

Single-Entry Bookkeeping

Single-entry bookkeeping is easiest to set up and maintain, though not all businesses can use it.

Most likely, you already have experience with single-entry bookkeeping. You use it when you balance your personal checking account, for example.

In this method, also known as cash basis accounting, you record income when you receive it, and you record expenses when you actually pay them. You do not include money that is owed to you but hasn't been received, or money that you owe but haven't paid.

If you have more income than expenses, you will have a positive balance. If you have more expenses than income, you will have a negative balance.

If the balance is negative, don't worry. The balance has little to do with your true profitability. It only shows what you have actually paid out or received for one month. You may have just closed a big deal but since your customer hasn't paid yet, the profits don't show up on paper.

In fact, you can expect your first few months to come up negative. It doesn't mean your business isn't sound, but rather that you are just starting and have more expenses than sources of income.

Not being able to see the relationship between cash flow and profitability is the critical disadvantage to single-entry bookkeeping. To get an accurate picture, you must use the slightly more complex double-entry method.

Double-Entry Bookkeeping

All double-entry accounting is based on the accounting equation:

Assets = Liabilities + Capital

Double-entry bookkeeping gets its name from the fact that for every business transaction made, entries must be made in at least two different accounts (one being a debit, the other a credit), and the total amounts must be equal.

What are debits and credits? When you set up an account, in either a journal or ledger, the format you use will be two columns. Debits are entered on the left-hand side, credits on the right. In accounting, the terms debit and credit do not have the traditional meanings associated with them in banking—a debit decreases your account while a credit increases it. It is very important to remember that in accounting, the terms mean nothing more than:

Debit = Left Column Entry
Credit = Right Column Entry

Journals

Journals are called books of original entry because they are the first place in which you record transactions. Later, you make entries recording the status of your accounts in ledgers, which are known as books of final entry. Your journals have two functions:

1. To provide a complete day-to-day record of similar transactions, classified under a common category.
2. To accumulate the results of daily transactions into periodic totals (usually monthly), so that these totals can be conveniently posted to the ledgers, the primary books of account.

Date	Transaction	Income Amount	Expense Amount
12/16/94	Electric Co.		$625.00
12/18/94	IBM	$2,628.00	
12/21/94	Phone Co.		$125.00

In a new business, you may need just one journal—the general journal—to accurately and thoroughly record transactions. As your business expands, you will need several, special journals.

Ledgers

Ledgers record increases and decreases in accounts. You use them to track your financial status.

Information from your journals is posted to your ledgers as often as possible. The ledger where you keep your asset, liability, and capital accounts is known as your general ledger.

Two excellent sources of computer software for managing your business are Quicken and Quick-Books, by Intuit.

WORKFORCE: INDEPENDENT CONTRACTORS OR EMPLOYEES?

According to James Wills, CPA, every individual who performs services subject to the will and control of an employer, both as to what shall be done and how it shall be done, is an employee for withholding tax purposes. It doesn't matter that the employee has considerable discretion and freedom of action, so long as the employer has the legal right to control both the method and result of the services.

It doesn't matter that the employee is designated a partner, agent, or independent contractor, or how the payments are measured or paid or what they are called.

A person not treated as an employee for tax purposes can't be covered under employee benefit plans, such as those for group insurance.

The Internal Revenue Service has a 20-factor test to use as a guide in determining whether a worker is an employee or an independent contractor. These factors help ascertain whether sufficient control is present to establish an employer-employee relationship. The 20 factors are:

1. A worker required to comply with others' instructions on when, where, and how to work is usually an employee.
2. Training a worker indicates control.
3. Integration of a worker's services into the business operations indicates control.
4. Services to be rendered personally and not delegated indicates control.
5. The right to hire, supervise, and pay assistants shows control.
6. A continuing relationship indicates an employment relationship.
7. Set hours of work for the worker indicates control.
8. Full-time work indicates control. An independent contractor is free to work when and for whom he or she chooses.
9. Work performed on a business's premises suggests control.
10. Requiring work be performed in a set order indicates control.
11. A requirement that the worker submit regular or written reports indicates control.
12. Payment by the hour, week, or month indicates an employment relationship.

13. Payment of business expenses indicates an employment relationship.
14. Furnishing of tools and equipment indicates an employment relationship.
15. Investment by the worker in facilities indicates an independent contractor.
16. The ability to realize a profit or loss from services indicates an independent contractor.
17. Working for more than one firm at a time indicates an independent contractor.
18. Services available to the general public on a regular and consistent basis indicates an independent contractor.
19. The right to discharge a worker indicates an employment relationship.
20. The worker's right to terminate his relationship without liability indicates an employment relationship.

If payment is made for services rendered and the payor is not sure whether the payee is an employee or an independent contractor, he or she can get an IRS ruling.

CHAPTER THIRTEEN

Building Your Public Image

"If you would not be forgotten as soon as you are dead, either write things worth reading or do things worth writing about."
BENJAMIN FRANKLIN

Chapter Chart

People have to know about your product or service to patronize your business. Through a combination of carefully selecting and building your image, drawing attention to your product or service and working hard to sell yourself and your dreams, you can develop a winning business.

- Developing an image for your business is an important way to communicate to customers what your work is all about.
- There are many forms of advertising, some more costly than others. A little strategy goes a long way toward helping you get your message out without emptying your pockets.
- Publicity is another way to attract attention to your work and your products. Learn how you can write your way into the public eye or get reporters to do it for you.

INTRODUCTION

People can't buy your product or service unless they know about it. And they won't buy it from you unless they have a good idea of what you and your company are like.

To get the customers you need, you have to draw attention to your product or service and carefully select and build your image. You have to work hard to sell yourself and your dreams.

WHAT'S YOUR IMAGE?

The key to finding the image that will sell your business is thinking about who your customers are. You probably have a few good ideas about these people from the market study we discussed in Chapter Four. What are your potential customers like; what are their needs, their interests and their desires?

You have to project yourself into the minds of your customers. Once you do that, you can develop an image that will be irresistible to them.

Developing an image is easier than it sounds. Think of a business you know, a pizza shop, for example. What's its image? Probably casual, fast and friendly. Now think of an antiques dealer: a totally different image—professional, exclusive and expensive.

BE CONSISTENT

Once you've found your market and worked out an image that sells, stick with it. If your market calls for a conservative image, go with it all the way. Don't hand out gray and navy business cards one day and fluorescent orange bumper stickers the next. People will get confused about what you stand for and will take their business to someone they feel they can trust.

Don't worry about laying it on too thick. The most successful organizations hold back nothing in promoting their business.

THE AD GAME

Good, old-fashioned word-of-mouth always has been, and always will be, the most effective advertising of all. In fact, other forms of advertising are only substitutes for word-of-mouth.

But you have to satisfy a few customers before they can go around bragging about how wonderful you are. How do you find these first few customers? Advertising. How do you keep your customer base growing while your customers brag about you? Advertising.

Since advertising will be a fact of life as long as you operate your business, you need to know how to get the most out of your dollar. It helps to know what kinds of advertising are available to help you spread your message.

A Guided Tour Of Advertising Media

When people talk about advertising, most think immediately of advertisements in newspapers or magazines. Advertising can also be telephone calls, banners on hot air balloons, handwritten letters, free pen-and-pencil sets and sales calls. In fact, anything can be a medium for advertising. Let's take a closer look at the options.

Direct Mail

In a direct mail campaign, you send a letter, brochure, catalogue or other printed material directly to people you think are interested in your product. You control exactly who gets the piece and you can offer a more detailed, reasoned pitch than you have space for in most other kinds of ads.

The drawback to direct mail is summed up in two words: junk mail. Many people assume that unsolicited mail is junk, and they throw away a large percentage of it unopened.

The trash factor notwithstanding, direct mail can be a powerful tool in a broad-based advertising campaign—especially if your business serves a specialized market. You can be reasonably certain, for example, that a tropical fish owner will read material promoting your new mail order company carrying merchandise for home aquariums.

The key to a successful direct mail campaign is narrowing the market to its thinnest slice. Then the people who get your material can't help but open the envelope and give your message a chance. When handled this way, direct marketing actually saves you money because you concentrate your ad dollars on the people who care most about your product.

Classified Ads

Classified ads provide an economical way of introducing your business to the community. Again, specialization is the key. Identify publications of interest to your target market. Anything from *Bee World,* the national magazine of beekeeping, to *Publisher's Weekly,* the national magazine of book publishing, can bring your specialized market to you.

Another variation on the classified ad is the display classified ad. Larger than a regular classified, it can be printed in boldface type, include your logo and have a border. These ads jump off a page of dull three-liners. For slightly more money than a regular classified, display classifieds capture the attention of all who glance across the page.

Display Ads

Display ads are the workhorse of the advertising world. They are useful because they convey information not only through words, but also through graphic design elements that give a sense of your overall image. Some advertisements convey relatively little solid information, giving themselves over completely to image and style.

The mix of information and style in your display ads should be balanced by your business's needs, the clientele you hope to attract, and your overall advertising strategy.

One particularly economical trick, good for new businesses on tight budgets, is to let your firm's business card double as a small display ad. This is especially effective if the business card contains a compelling graphic, such as a line drawing or an interesting typeface, as part of the design.

It's often useful to include a coupon in your advertisement. By far the most common is the "Send for your free brochure/catalog" variety. This device is very effective because anyone who sends in the coupon is a promising candidate for a sale and a good target for further promotional efforts such as direct mail.

Radio and Television

Be prepared to spend big if you want to use radio or television. Though costly, these media have a lot to offer your advertising effort. They reach many more consumers in one run than printed media can. They also have snob appeal. People know these ads are expensive, so broadcast advertising lends prestige to your operation.

It's important to remember that broadcast ads reach a diverse audience. If your product appeals to a specialized market, you may be wasting money giving your pitch to thousands who won't respond. Make sure that broadcast ads will work for you before you spend your cash.

Telemarketing

Telemarketing is a form of advertising done over the telephone. Salespeople call individuals likely to be interested in your product or service and talk to them about what you have to offer.

Because this form of advertising involves direct interaction between a salesperson and a potential customer, it can be very effective. If the customer has misgivings or questions about your product or service, the salesperson can alleviate those doubts. If you want to emphasize certain aspects of your business—your superior warranty and return policy, for example—the sales staff can play up this part of your pitch.

Since the advent of the computer, a machine can sit at a desk, dial telephone numbers and deliver your spiel about your products and services. All the programming in the world, however, can't make the computer an eloquent, charming salesperson. Don't be tempted by lower cost into using automated telemarketers.

Location Ads

Location ads include posters, billboards and signs strategically located where large numbers of people will see them. This type of ad must be very noticeable—otherwise people will tune it out. Some business owners use the same artwork and design in both space ads and location ads. Not only does this save money, it also makes it easier for the public to associate a certain image with your business.

The crucial factor in developing a location ad is the location itself. How many people can see the advertisment without going out of their way? Another important factor is the length of time your ad will stay in place. Your ad works much harder for you the longer you let it remain because more people have a chance to see it more times.

You see an effective location for advertising every day—the grounds of your business itself. If your building is visible to passersby, you could put a sign or awning outside to announce your business. Not only will you advertise your business, you'll also show that it is right there, where people practically trip over it on their way to other places.

The Trinkets of the Trade

Another time-tested method of advertising consists of handing out small articles that people use every day—matchbooks, pens, coffee cups, calendars and key chains that have your logo on them. Every time someone uses the article they will be reminded of your business.

It makes good marketing sense to match the trinket with the market you're going after.

The Yellow Pages

Probably the best bargain around for advertising is the one most often taken for granted: the Yellow Pages. Your business will have long-term exposure at a reasonable cost.

First, it reaches nearly every household, and it neatly guides consumers in search of your product or service directly to your ad. Second, your ad works for an entire year. Third, you won't find a less expensive space anywhere. So by all means, let their fingers do the walking!

The Personal Approach

As chief executive officer of your company, you have a lot of clout. You can use that clout in personal sales calls to well-targeted potential customers. Establishing a warm personal connection with key people practically guarantees that they will choose your firm when they need a product or service that you offer.

Don't use this contact to make a hard sales pitch. Instead, establish a business relationship, find out firsthand just what your potential customers need, and show them that your company is positioned to answer that need.

If you use this approach, keep a couple of points in mind. First, you have to be polished. If you're nervous or disorganized, you look like an amateur.

Second, make sure you're getting to the people who count. If your business is drafting supplies, present yourself to the art department, not to the receptionist. If, on the other hand, you have a courier service to sell, go straight to the secretaries who make the decisions about which courier to use.

STRATEGY AND YOUR BUDGET

There's more to advertising than merely throwing dollars at a newspaper, television station or telemarketing company. You have to know how to make each dollar work as hard as possible to bring your customers to you. Sound advertising strategy helps you make the most of your advertising budget and strengthens your image within your market.

Diversity

If you diversify, you hedge your bets on every ad you buy. If you sink your entire advertising budget into one space ad, and it is unsuccessful, you're out of money—and luck. It is better to combine a number of different types of ads in a well-planned campaign. If one ad doesn't work, you will have others that may.

> *"Don't make the mistake of believing you get only one chance to reach your potential customer, or that each package or advertisement must tell everything. Much better to proceed as though you are beginning a long dialogue with your customer. Write copy that respects this relationship."*
>
> PAUL HAWKFEN, *GROWING A BUSINESS*

Cost-effectiveness

You can spend $70 to get your name in the Yellow Pages or $15,000 for a 30-second spot on your local television network. How can you tell if the larger price tag is worth it? You need to look at two major factors: cost and effectiveness.

When thinking about effectiveness keep in mind the factors that can make or break your ad:

How many people will see it?
How often will they see it?
Will they respond to it?

The greater the number of people who see your ad, the greater the number who will be able to respond. Consider the billboard on your local thoroughfare or the half-page ad next to your local T.V. listings. Hundreds, perhaps thousands, of people see these ads on a given day. Think of the results if just 1% of these people respond to the ad.

Repetition

Research has shown that people like something better the more they're exposed to it. Repetition, therefore, is a cornerstone of successful advertising.

You achieve repetition by leaving your ad somewhere for a period of time. If you're running a display ad in your local newspaper, for example, run it for four issues instead of just one. Each time readers see it, they are one step closer to becoming your customers.

If your ad is on a billboard or poster slot, leave it there for several months. Let it penetrate the minds of passersby so that one day, when they need your product or service, they automatically turn to your company.

The Punch Factor

For an ad to sell, it has to have punch. It has to win people's attention over the messages of your competitors. Think about some ads you've seen lately. Chances are, you remember only one or two of the hundreds you've been exposed to. For your money, wouldn't you like your ad to be memorable?

PUBLICITY—READ IT IN THE PAPERS

The power of advertising is hard to dispute. But sometimes even advertising isn't enough. You can get an edge on the competition by combining advertising with well-placed publicity.

Publicity, unlike advertising, is free. Also unlike advertising, publicity is considered unbiased, for the simple reason that it comes out of editorial departments, under the careful review of editors who aren't on your payroll.

The best publicity comes from feature articles in local newspapers and magazines. Either you write the article yourself or you get a reporter to write it for you. Though it can be tricky to get a reporter involved, with a little savvy you can have all the coverage you need.

Feature Articles

As someone whose life is devoted to the business you run, you are an expert. You may take your know-how for granted, but what you know is valuable to other people.

Suppose, for example, your business is dry cleaning. You know a lot about fabric care, stain removal and quality treatment for long lasting wear and durability.

To get publicity, you could write an article on what you know for your neighborhood newspaper. Two or three double-spaced pages would be plenty. Readers of the article would get the impression that you know what you're talking about, and they would feel comfortable trusting their clothing to your capable hands.

Almost any kind of business has a story idea in it. Heating oil and gas entrepreneurs could write about saving energy or keeping furnaces running properly. Hairdressers could write about caring for color-treated or permed hair, or for summer readers, minimizing sun damage at the beach. The possibilities are endless!

News Events

You can get free publicity by having a reporter write an article for you.

To do this, you need to create a situation that would be interesting to the local press. In publicity circles, this is called creating news.

Community service makes great news and has the added benefit of making you look benevolent. Sponsor a fundraising dinner for a local volunteer organization. Organize a marathon to benefit a health organization. Give your employees a few hours off each month to care for the homeless.

If community service doesn't appeal to you, try doing something outrageous. Get a tightrope walker to put on a show in front of your store. Start a controversy by taking an unusual stand on issues of importance in your community.

There's always something that begs doing. If you're the one to do it, you can attract the attention of reporters in your area.

Presentations and Lectures

Another way to get publicity, used successfully by a wide variety of business people, is to give lectures and classes to groups in your area. If you're a bicycle retailer, you could teach an adult education course on basic bike maintenance. Real estate agents could teach about first-time home buying. Travel agents could give lectures on international currency exchange and unusual vacations.

You could also make presentations to amateur and professional groups in your area. If you are in retail clothing, you might give a workshop on "The Look of Success" to local chapters of executive or business organizations. Child care entrepreneurs could talk about after-school care to a chapter of the local PTA. The possibilities are endless, and they eventually add up to money in the bank for you.

The End Result

You probably have generated a number of ideas for promoting your business while reading this chapter. Take a minute to jot these down. Your next step is to show your ideas to a professional who can advise you on the best combination of advertising and promotion for your needs. Then get ready to see your business's name in lights!

BUILDING YOUR PUBLIC IMAGE STEP-BY-STEP

1. What image do you want your business to have? Make your decision based on:
   - The type of business you have
   - Your target area
   - Your target customers
2. Once you've decided . . .
   - Be consistent
   - Promote, promote, promote
3. Advertising options
   - Newspapers, magazines, etc.
   - Television, radio
   - Direct mail
   - Display ads
   - Classified ads
   - Business cards, printed pencils, cups, T-shirts, etc.
   - Catalogues, brochures
   - Telemarketing
   - Signs, posters, billboards
   - Yellow Pages and other directories
4. Publicity
   - Feature articles
   - News events
   - Presentations and lectures

Afterword

From the time we are very small, most of us are continually told that we cannot do certain things. This book, however, tells you that if you are willing to follow established guidelines and if you have the determination and energy, you can start your own business.

Beginning a business is a widely sought-after goal for those in the corporate world, retired people, or even those who are new to the working world.

This book is designed to start you thinking in the right direction. Use it, mark it up and make your dream come alive.

It is our belief that Henry David Thoreau summed it up with these words:

> "If one advances confidently in the direction of his own dreams and endeavors, to live the life that he himself has imagined, he will be met with a success unknown in common hours."

Entrepreneur Boot Camp is like a road sign that points your way to success. At this juncture in your reading, you have gained the benefit of years of business experience, saving yourself from having to learn what works and what doesn't on your own.

Now you're educated. The rest is up to you. You need to do more than reading and thinking and planning. You need to start doing.

We encourage you to write us with your stories and suggestions. Point your way to success with this book.

The Dreamers
Jerry Perone and Arnold Sanow

APPENDIX ONE

Start-Your-Own-Business Kit

YOUR BUSINESS SUCCESS CHECKLIST

Getting Started

YOUR BUILDING

Have you found a good building for your store? ______

Will you have enough room when your business gets bigger? ______

Can you fix the building the way you want it without spending too much money? ______

Can people get to it easily from parking spaces, bus stops, or their homes? ______

Have you had a lawyer check the lease and zoning? ______

EQUIPMENT AND SUPPLIES

Do you know just what equipment and supplies you need and how much they will cost? ______

Can you save some money by buying second-hand equipment? ______

YOUR MERCHANDISE

Have you decided what things you will sell? ______

Do you know how much or how many of each you will buy to open your store with? ______

Have you found suppliers who will sell you what you need at a good price? ______

Have you compared the prices and credit terms of different suppliers? ______

YOUR RECORDS

Have you planned a system of records that will keep track of your income and expenses, what you owe other people, and what other people owe you? ______

Have you worked out a way to keep track of your inventory so that you will always have enough on hand for your customers but not more than you can sell? ______

Have you figured out how to keep your payroll records and take care of tax reports and payments? ______

Do you know what financial statements you should prepare? ______

Do you know an accountant who will help you with your records and financial statements? ______

YOUR STORE AND THE LAW

Do you know what licenses and permits you need? ______

Do you know what business laws you have to obey? ______

Do you know a lawyer you can go to for advice and for help with legal papers? ______

PROTECTING YOUR STORE

Have you made plans for protecting your store against thefts of all kinds—shoplifting, robbery, burglary, employee stealing? ______

Have you talked with an insurance agent about what kinds of insurance you need? ______

BUYING A BUSINESS SOMEONE ELSE HAS STARTED

Have you made a list of what you like and don't like about buying a business someone else has started? ______

Are you sure you know the real reason why the owner wants to sell this business? ______

Have you compared the cost of buying the business with the cost of starting a new business? ______

Is the stock up to date and in good condition? _______

Is the building in good condition? _______

Will the owner of the building transfer the lease to you? _______

Have you talked with other business owners in the area to see what they think of the business? _______

Have you talked with the company's suppliers? _______

Have you talked with a lawyer about it? _______

Making It Go

ADVERTISING

Have you decided how you will advertise? (Newspapers—posters—handbills—radio—mail) _______

Do you know where to get help with your ads? _______

Have you watched what other stores do to get people to buy? _______

THE PRICES YOU CHARGE

Do you know how to figure what you should charge for each item you sell? _______

Do you know what other stores like yours charge? _______

BUYING

Do you have a plan for finding out what your customers want? _______

Will your plan for keeping track of your inventory tell you when it is time to order more and how much to order? _______

Do you plan to buy most of your stock from a few suppliers rather than a little from many, so that those you buy from will want to help you succeed? _______

SELLING

Have you decided whether you will have salesclerks or self-service? _______

Do you know how to get customers to buy? _______

Have you thought about why you like to buy from some salesclerks while others turn you off? ______

YOUR EMPLOYEES

If you need to hire someone to help you, do you know where to look? ______

Do you know what kind of person you need? ______

Do you have a plan for training your employees? ______

CREDIT FOR YOUR CUSTOMERS

Have you decided whether or not to let your customers buy on credit? ______

Do you know the good and bad points about joining a credit-card plan? ______

Can you tell a deadbeat from a good credit customer? ______

A FEW EXTRA QUESTIONS

Have you figured out whether or not you could make more money working for someone else? ______

Does your family go along with your plan to start a business of your own? ______

Do you know where to find out about new ideas and new products? ______

Do you have a work plan for yourself and your employees? ______

Have you gone to the nearest Small Business Administration office for help with your plans? ______

If you have answered all these questions carefully, you've done some hard work and serious thinking. That's good. But you have probably found some things you still need to know more about or do something about.

Do all you can for yourself, but don't hesitate to ask for help from people who can tell you what you need to know. Remember, running a business takes guts! You've got to be able to decide what you need and then go after it. Good luck!

CORPORATION PAPERWORK AND FORMALITIES CHECKLIST

A Self Examination of Your Corporation's Health

The following checklist is a convenient way for you to check the health of your corporation. If you don't yet have a corporation, you can use this list to assist in setting it up. We suggest that you check the question only when you are completely confident with the answer. The more checks you have, the better your corporation's health. Questions with asterisks next to them are critical to your liability and tax protection. The other questions are important too, but those with asterisks are VITAL! (This checklist was developed by Laughlin Associates of Carson City, NV, 1-800-648-0966.)

1. Have you read and do you fully understand your Articles of Incorporation? ______
2. Have you signed an Acceptance of Appointment as Director and included it in your corporate records? ______
3. Have you properly filled out the Resolution which elects and appoints additional Directors of your corporation if you have them, and filed it in your corporate records? ______
4. Have these additional directors signed an Acceptance of Appointment as Director? ______ ***
5. Have you held a first Board of Directors meeting? ______ ***
6. Do you have proper and adequate minutes for the first meeting of the Board of Directors of your corporation? ______
7. Has your corporation decided on a fiscal year? ______

8. Have the Directors of your corporation elected officers? ______
9. Has a Stock Ledger Statement been filled out by the secretary of the corporation? ______
10. Have by-laws for your corporation been adopted by your Board of Directors or shareholders? ______ ***
11. Have you made sure that proper notice was given for any board meetings held or an appropriate waiver executed? ______
12. Has the board of your corporation authorized the issuance of the corporation's stock? ______ ***
13. Has your corporation issued stock yet? ______ ***
14. If any stock has been issued, was it issued pursuant to a properly executed corporate resolution? ______
15. Do you fully understand your corporation's by-laws? ______
16. Do you understand what is covered by the by-laws and what is covered by the Articles of Incorporation and how they relate? ______
17. Have the stock issues of your corporation been recorded properly in your corporate record stock ledger book? ______
18. Have the officers that the board elected accepted their election as officers? ______

19. Has the corporation secured a federal tax ID number from the IRS? ______

20. Do you know if your corporation is legally doing business in another state? ______

21. Have you made sure to file all necessary filings in any state in which your corporation is legally doing business? ______ ***

22. If your corporation is near or over a year old, have you had an annual meeting of your shareholders? ______ ***

23. If your corporation is near or over a year old have you had an annual meeting of the board? ______

24. Have you given proper notice, or used the appropriate waiver of notice, for all meetings of stockholders or Directors? ______ ***

25. Have you been sure to have proper minutes for all meetings of shareholders and Directors? ______

26. Have you been sure to use a corporate resolution of the board to authorize and document all major corporate acts? ______ ***

27. Have you been sure to keep separate books and bank accounts for the corporation and yourself, making sure at all times never to commingle any funds? ______ ***

28. Are you sure that your tax returns, books of accounts and corporate record book all say the same thing? ______ ***

29. Are you sure that you have properly documented all transactions between you and the corporation with resolutions, minutes, etc.? ______ ***
30. On every document that you have executed, have you done so on behalf of the corporation *as its officer* by signing with your title, to guard against any personal liability? ______ ***
31. Do you have a resolution authorizing the opening of a bank account, naming the institution and the signatory(ies)? ______
32. Was your corporation properly capitalized? ______ ***
33. Have you documented all transactions between related parties and the corporation with resolutions, notes, contracts, etc.? ______
34. Do you have a resolution documenting the business purposes for any questionable deductions? ______ ***
35. Are you totally current on the above corporate formalities? ______
36. Has your corporation adopted an official promissory note for corporate use? ______
37. Has your corporation adopted an official expense account for official corporate use that meets IRS guidelines? ______
38. If you haven't performed the above items, do you know how to bring your records up to date? ______

LETTER TO SECRETARY OF STATE REQUESTING RESERVATION OF CORPORATE NAME

______________________________ , 1995

Secretary of State

____

____

____

RE: Reservation of Corporate Name

This letter is your formal authorization to reserve the first available corporate name, in the order in which they appear below:

1.

2.

3.

Also enclosed is a check in the amount of $__________ to cover the reservation fee. Please acknowledge and confirm which corporate name has been reserved for me for a period of at least ninety (90) days.

Regards,

____

(Signature)
(Typed or printed name)

TRANSMITTAL LETTER FOR FILING ARTICLES OF INCORPORATION

______________________________ , 1995

Secretary of State

____

____

____

RE: Filing of Articles of Incorporation

Please find enclosed an original and _________ copies of the Articles of Incorporation for filing. Also enclosed is a check in the amount of $__________ to cover the filing fees and costs associated with this submittal, as well as a stamped, self-addressed envelope.

Please return to me one or more conformed copies of the Articles of Incorporation in the enclosed stamped, self-addressed envelope.

If you have any questions or require additional information, please write or call me at (_____) ______ - _________.

Regards,

____

(Signature)
(Typed or printed name)

ARTICLES OF INCORPORATION OF

____

ARTICLE I—NAME

The name of the corporation is ______________________________.

ARTICLE II—PURPOSE

The purpose of the corporation is to engage in any lawful act or activity for which a corporation may be organized under the applicable General Corporation Law of the State of ____________________, other than ____________________

____

ARTICLE III—AGENT FOR SERVICE OF PROCESS

The name and address in this state of the corporation's initial agent for service of process is

ARTICLE IV—CAPITAL STOCK

The maximum number of shares of stock that this corporation is authorized to have outstanding at any one time is __________ shares of common stock having a par value of $__________ per share.

ARTICLE V—LIMITATION OF LIABILITY

Each director, stockholder, and officer, in consideration for his services, shall, in the absence of fraud, intentional misconduct, or a knowing violation of the law, be indemnified, whether then in office or not, for the reasonable cost and expenses incurred by him in connection with the defense of, or for advice concerning any claim asserted or proceeding brought against him by reason of his being or having been a director, stockholder or officer of the corporation or of any subsidiary of the corporation, whether or not wholly owned, to the maximum extent permitted by law. The foregoing right of indemnification shall be inclusive of any other rights to which any director, stockholder or officer may be entitled as a matter of law.

ARTICLE VI—INCORPORATOR

The name and address of the incorporator is ____________________

____

IN WITNESS WHEREOF, the undersigned has executed these Articles of Incorporation on this _________ day of ________________________, 1995.

INCORPORATOR:	INCORPORATOR:
By: ______________________________	By: ______________________________
(Signature)	(Signature)
(Typed or printed name)	(Typed or printed name)

STATE OF ____________________________

COUNTY OF __________________________ }ss

On ____ before me, ____, personally appeared ____, personally known to me (or proved to me on the basis of satisfactory evidence) to be the person(s) whose name(s) is/are subscribed to the within instrument and acknowledged to me that he/she/they executed the same in his/her/their authorized capacity(ies) and that by his/her/their signature(s) on the instrument the person(s) or the entity upon behalf of which the person(s) acted, executed the instrument.

WITNESS my hand and official seal.

____

(Signature)

BYLAWS
OF

____

ARTICLE I
OFFICES

Section 1. PRINCIPAL OFFICE. The principal office for the transaction of business of the corporation is hereby fixed and located at ____________________, City of ________________________, County of ________________________, State of ________________________. The location may be changed by approval of a majority of the authorized Directors, and additional offices may be established and maintained at such other place or places, as the Board of Directors may from time to time designate.

Section 2. OTHER OFFICES. Branch or subordinate offices may at any time be established by the Board of Directors at any place or places where the corporation is qualified to do business.

ARTICLE II
SHAREHOLDERS

Section 1. ANNUAL MEETINGS. The annual meeting of the shareholders of this Corporation shall be held at _________.m. on the __________________ day of ________________________ of each year or at such other time and place designated by the Board of Directors of the Corporation. Business transacted at the annual meeting shall include the election of Directors of the Corporation and all other matters properly before the Board. If the designated day shall fall on a Sunday or legal holiday, the meeting shall be held on the first business day thereafter.

Section 2. SPECIAL MEETINGS. Special meetings of the shareholders may be called at any time by the Board of Directors, the Chairman of the Board, the President, a Vice President, the Secretary, or by one or more shareholders holding not less than one-tenth (1/10) of the voting power of the corporation. Except as next provided, notice shall be given as for the annual meeting.

Upon receipt of a written request addressed to the Chairman, President, Vice President, or Secretary, mailed or delivered personally to such Officer by any person (other than the Board) entitled to call a special meeting of shareholders, such Officer shall cause notice to be given, to the shareholders entitled to vote, that a meeting will be held at a time requested by the person or persons calling the meeting, not less than ten (10) nor more than sixty (60) days after the receipt of such request or as required by state statute. If such notice is not given within twenty (20) days, or as required by state statute, after receipt of such request, the persons calling the meeting may give notice thereof in the manner provided by these Bylaws.

Section 3. Place of Meetings. The Board of Directors may designate any place, either within or without the State of ________________________________, as the place of meeting for any annual meeting or for any special meeting called by the Board of Directors. A waiver of notice signed before the meeting by all shareholders entitled to vote at a meeting may designate any place as the place for the holding of such meeting. If no designation is made, or if a special meeting be otherwise called, the place of meeting shall be the principal office of the Corporation.

Section 4. Notice of Meetings. Notice of meetings, annual or special, shall be given in writing not less than ten (10) nor more than sixty (60) days before the date of the meeting, or as required by state statute, to shareholders entitled to vote thereat. Such notice shall be given by the Secretary or the Assistant Secretary, or if there be no such Officer, or in the case of his or her neglect or refusal, by any Director or shareholder.

Notice of any meeting of shareholders shall specify the place, the day and the hour of meeting, and (1) in case of a special meeting, the general nature of the business to be transacted and no other business may be transacted, or (2) in the case of an annual meeting, those matters which the Board at date of mailing intends to present for action by the shareholders. At any meetings where Directors are to be elected, notice shall include the names of the nominees, if any, intended at date of notice to be presented by management for election.

If a shareholder supplies no address, notice shall be deemed to have been given if mailed to the place where the principal executive office of the Corporation is situated, or published at least once in some newspaper of general circulation in the county of said principal office.

Notice shall be deemed given at the time it is delivered personally or deposited in the mail or sent by other means of written communication. The Officer giving such notice or report shall prepare and file an affidavit or declaration thereof.

Section 5. Adjourned Meetings and Notice Thereof. Any shareholders' meeting, annual or special, whether or not a quorum is present, may be adjourned from time to time by the vote of a majority of the shares, the holders of which are either present in person or represented by proxy thereat, but in the absence of a quorum no other business may be transacted at any such meeting.

When any shareholders' meeting, either annual or special, is adjourned for thirty (30) days or more, notice of the adjourned meeting shall be given as in the case of an original meeting. If the meeting is adjourned for less than thirty (30) days, it shall not be necessary to give any notice of the time and place of the adjourned meeting or of the business to be transacted thereat, other than by announcement at the meeting at which such adjournment is taken.

Section 6. Entry of Notice. An entry in the minutes of any meeting of shareholders to the effect that notice has been duly given shall be prima facie evidence that due notice of such meeting was given to all shareholders as required by law and by these Bylaws.

Section 7. Closing of Transfer Books for Fixing of Record Date. For the purpose of determining shareholders entitled to notice of or to vote at any meeting of shareholders or any adjournment thereof, or shareholders entitled to receive payment of any dividend, or in order to make a determination of shareholders for any other proper purpose, the Board of Directors of the Corporation may provide that the stock transfer books shall be closed for a stated period, but not to exceed in any case fifty (50) days. If the stock transfer books shall be closed for the purpose of determining shareholders entitled to notice of or to vote at a meeting of shareholders, such books shall be closed for at least ten (10) days immediately preceding such meeting.

In lieu of closing the stock transfer books, the Board of Directors may fix in advance a date as the record date for any such determination of shareholders, such date in any case to be not more than fifty (50) days and, in case of a meeting of shareholders, not less than ten (10) days prior to the date on which the particular action, requiring such determination of shareholders, is to be taken. If the stock transfer books are not closed and no record date is fixed for the determination of shareholders entitled to notice of or to vote at a meeting of shareholders, or shareholders entitled to receive payment of a dividend, the date on which notice of the meeting is mailed or the date on which the resolution of the Board of Directors declaring such dividend is adopted, as the case may be, shall be the record date for such determination of shareholders. If the above chosen dates do not comply with applicable state statutes or the state of incorporation, such dates shall be modified to so comply.

When a determination of shareholders entitled to vote at any meeting of shareholders has been made as provided in this section, such determination shall apply to any adjournment thereof except where the determination has been made through the closing of the stock transfer books and the stated period of closing has expired.

Section 8. Waiver of Notice or Consent by Absent Shareholders. The transactions of any meeting of shareholders, however called and noticed, shall be valid as though had at a meeting duly held after regular call and notice, if a quorum be present either in person or by proxy, and if, either before or after the meeting, each of the shareholders entitled to vote, not present in person or by proxy, sign a written waiver of notice, or a consent to the holding of such meeting or an approval of the minutes thereof. All such waivers, consents or approvals shall be filed with the corporate records or made a part of the minutes of the meeting.

Section 9. Shareholders Acting Without a Meeting. Any action which may be taken at a meeting of the shareholders may be taken without a meeting or notice of meeting if authorized by a writing signed by all (or by such lesser percentage as may be authorized by law) of the shareholders entitled to vote at a meeting for such purposes, and filed with the Secretary of the Corporation.

Section 10. Quorum. The holders of a majority of the shares entitled to vote thereat, present in person or represented by proxy, shall constitute a quorum at all meetings of the shareholders for the transaction of business except as otherwise provided by law, by the Articles of Incorporation, or by these By-laws. If, however, such majority shall not be present or represented at any meeting of the shareholders, the shareholders entitled to vote thereat, present in person or by proxy, shall have the power to adjourn the meeting from time to time, until the requisite amount of voting shares shall be present. At such adjourned meeting at which the requisite amount of voting shares shall be represented, any business may be transacted which might have been transacted at a meeting as originally notified.

If a quorum be initially present, the shareholders may continue to transact business until adjournment, notwithstanding the withdrawal of enough shareholders to leave less than a quorum, if any action taken is approved by a majority of the shareholders required to initially constitute a quorum.

Section 11. VOTING—IN GENERAL. Only persons in whose names shares entitled to vote stand on the stock records of the Corporation on the day of any meeting of shareholders, unless some other day be fixed by the Board of Directors for the determination of shareholders of record, and then on such other day, shall be entitled to vote at such meeting.

Provided the candidate's name has been placed in nomination prior to the voting and one or more shareholder has given notice at the meeting prior to the voting of the shareholder's intent to cumulate the shareholder's votes, every shareholder entitled to vote at any election for Directors of any Corporation for profit may cumulate their votes and give one candidate a number of votes equal to the number of Directors to be elected multiplied by the number of votes to which his or her shares are entitled, or distribute his or her votes on the same principle among as many candidates as he or she thinks fit.

The candidates receiving the highest number of votes up to the number of Directors to be elected are elected.

Section 12. VOTING BY CERTAIN HOLDERS. Shares outstanding in the name of another Corporation may be voted by such officer, agent or proxy as the Bylaws of such Corporation may prescribe, or, in the absence of such provision, as the Board of Directors of such Corporation may determine.

Shares held by an administrator, executor, guardian, or conservator may be voted by him or her, either in person or by proxy, without a transfer of such shares into their name. Shares standing in the name of a trustee may be voted by him or her, either in person or by proxy, but no trustee shall be entitled to vote shares held by them without a transfer of such shares into the name of the Trust.

Shares standing in the name of a receiver may be voted by such receiver, and shares held by or under the control of a receiver may be voted by such receiver without the transfer thereof into his name if authority to do so is contained in an appropriate order of the court by which such receiver was appointed.

A shareholder whose shares are pledged shall be entitled to vote such shares until the shares have been transferred into the name of the pledge, and thereafter the pledgee shall be entitled to vote the shares so transferred.

Section 13. INSPECTORS OF ELECTION. Before any shareholders' meeting, the Board of Directors may appoint any persons, other than nominees for office, to act as inspectors of election at the meeting or its adjournment. If no inspectors of election are appointed, the Chairman of the meeting may, and on the request of any shareholder or his proxy shall, appoint inspectors of election at the meeting. The number of inspectors shall be either one (1) or three (3). If inspectors are appointed at a meeting on the request of one or more shareholders or proxies, the holders of a majority of shares or their proxies present at the meeting shall determine whether one (1) or three (3) inspectors are to be appointed. If any person appointed as inspector fails to appear or fails or refuses to act, the vacancy may be filled by appointment by the Board of Directors before the meeting, or by the Chairman at the meeting.

The duties of these inspectors shall be as prescribed under applicable law and shall include:

(A) determining the number of shares outstanding and the voting power of each, the shares represented at the meeting, the existence of a quorum, and the authenticity, validity, and effect of proxies;
(B) receiving votes, ballots, or consents;
(C) hearing and determining all challenges and questions in any way arising in connection with the right to vote;
(D) counting and tabulating all votes or consents;
(E) determining the election result; and
(F) any other acts that may be proper to conduct the election or vote with fairness to all shareholders.

Section 14. Proxies. Every person entitled to vote or execute consents shall have the right to do so either in person or by one or more agents authorized by a written proxy executed by the person or his authorized agent and filed with the Secretary of the Corporation. A validly executed proxy shall continue in full force and effect until an instrument revoking it or a new valid proxy bearing a later date is filed with the Secretary of the Corporation, provided that no proxy shall be valid after eleven (11) months from the date of its continued execution, unless the proxy specifies the length of time for which it is to continue in force, which in no event shall exceed seven (7) years from the date of its execution.

Section 15. Organization. The President, or in the absence of the President, any Vice President, shall call the meeting of the shareholders to order and shall act as Chairman of the meeting. In the absence of the President and all of the Vice Presidents, shareholders shall appoint a Chairman for such meeting. The Secretary of the Corporation shall act as Secretary of all meetings of the shareholders, but in the absence of the Secretary at any meeting of the shareholders, the presiding Officer may appoint any person to act as Secretary of the meeting.

ARTICLE III
DIRECTORS

Section 1. Powers. Subject to limitations in the Articles of Incorporation and applicable law on actions that must be authorized or approved by the shareholders, and subject to the duties of Directors as prescribed by these Bylaws, all corporate powers shall be exercised by or under the authority of, and the Corporation's business and affairs shall be controlled by the Board of Directors. By way of illustration and not in limitation of those powers, the Board of Directors shall have authority to:

(A) select and remove at pleasure all officers, agents and employees of the Corporation, prescribe such powers and duties for them as may not be inconsistent with law with the Articles of Incorporation or with these Bylaws, fix their compensation, and require from them security for faithful service;

(B) conduct, manage and control the affairs and business of the Corporation and make such rules and regulations therefore not inconsistent with law, with the Articles of Incorporation or with these Bylaws, as they may deem best;

(C) change the principal office for the transaction of the business of the Corporation from one location to another within the same county as provided in Article I hereof; fix and locate from time to time one or more subsidiary offices of the Corporation; designate any place for the holding of any shareholders' meeting or meetings; and adopt, make and use a corporate seal, and prescribe the form of certificate of stock, and alter the form of such seal and of such certificates from time to time, as in their judgment they may deem best, provided such seal and such certificates shall at all times comply with the applicable provisions of law;

(D) authorize the issuance of shares of stock of the Corporation from time to time, upon such terms as may be lawful, in consideration of money paid, labor done or services actually rendered, debts or securities canceled, tangible or intangible property actually received, or such other consideration as may be authorized by law;

(E) borrow money and incur indebtedness for the purposes of the Corporation, and cause to be executed and delivered therefor, in the corporate name, promissory notes, bonds, debentures, deeds of trust, mortgages, pledges, hypothecations or other evidences of debt and securities therefor;

(F) adopt and administer, or provide for the administration of, employee stock purchase plans, employee stock option plans, employee stock bonus plans, and any other plans or arrangements whereby Directors, Officers, employees or agent of the Corporation or any other entity may be entitled to acquire authorized but unissued or treasury stock or other securities of the Corporation, upon such terms and conditions as may from time to time be permitted by law;

(G) declare dividends out of funds legally available therefor, whenever, in their sound discretion, such action is warranted;

(H) amend, alter, or repeal the Bylaws of the Corporation, or adopt new Bylaws as hereinafter provided; and

(I) generally do and perform every act and thing whatsoever that may pertain to the office of the Directors, and exercise all the powers and perform all the acts which the Corporation can legally exercise and perform under its Articles of Incorporation.

Section 2. Standard of Care. Each Director shall perform the duties of a Director, including the duties as a member of any committee of the Board upon which the Director may serve, in good faith, in a manner such Director believes to be in the best interests of the Corporation, and with such care, including reasonable inquiry, as an ordinary prudent person in a like position would use under similar circumstances.

Section 3. **NUMBER AND QUALIFICATIONS OF DIRECTORS.** The authorized number of Directors shall be ____________________ (_____). The number of Directors may be increased or decreased from time to time by amendment to these Bylaws; provided, however, that the number shall never be less than ______ , and provided further that no decrease in the number of Directors shall have the effect of shortening the term of any incumbent Director. Directors need not be residents of the State of ________________________________ nor shareholders of _________________________ the Corporation.

Section 4. **ELECTION AND TERM OF OFFICE.** The Directors shall be elected at each annual shareholders' meeting; however, if any annual meeting is not held or the Directors are not elected at any annual meeting, they may be elected at any special shareholders' meeting held for that purpose. Each Director shall hold office until his successor is elected. Director, including a Director elected to fill a vacancy, shall hold office until the expiration of the term for which elected and until a successor has been elected and qualified.

Section 5. **VACANCIES.** Vacancies in the Board of Directors may be filled by a majority of the remaining Directors, though less than a quorum, or by a sole remaining Director, except that a vacancy created by the removal of a Director by the vote or written consent of the shareholders or by court order may be filled only by the vote of a majority of the shares entitled to vote represented at a duly held meeting at which a quorum is present, or by the written consent of holders of a majority of the outstanding shares entitled to vote. Each Director so elected shall hold office until the next annual meeting of the shareholders and until a successor has been elected and qualified.

A vacancy or vacancies in the Board of Directors shall be deemed to exist in the event of the death, resignation, or removal of any Director, or if the Board of Directors by resolution declares vacant the office of a Director who has been declared of unsound mind by an order of court or convicted of a felony, or if the authorized number of Directors is increased, or if the shareholders fail, at any meeting of shareholders at which any Director or Directors are elected, to elect the number of Directors to be voted for at that meeting.

The shareholders may elect a Director or Directors at any time to fill any vacancy or vacancies not filled by the Directors, but any such election by written consent shall require the consent of a majority of the outstanding shares entitled to vote.

No reduction of the authorized number of Directors shall have the effect of removing any Director before that Director's term of office expires.

If the Board of Directors accepts the resignation of a Director tendered to take effect at a future time, the Board or the shareholders may elect a successor to take office when the resignation is to become effective.

Section 6. **REMOVAL OF DIRECTORS.** The entire Board of Directors or any individual Director may be removed from office as provided by state law. In such case the remaining Board members may elect a successor Director to fill such vacancy for the remaining unexpired term of the Director so removed.

Section 7. Notice, Place and Manner of Meetings. Meetings of the Board of Directors may be called by the Chairman of the Board, or the President, or any Vice President, or the Secretary, or any two (2) Directors (or one (1) Director if there is only one (1) Director) and shall be held at the principal executive office of the Corporation, unless some other place is designated in the notice of the meeting. Members of the Board may participate in a meeting through use of a conference telephone or similar communications equipment so long as all members participating in such a meeting can hear one another. Accurate minutes of any meeting of the Board or any committee thereof shall be maintained by the Secretary or other Officer designated for that purpose.

Section 8. Organization Meetings. The organization meetings of the Board of Directors shall be held at the corporate offices, or such other place as may be designated by the Board of Directors.

Section 9. Other Regular Meetings. Regular meetings of the Board of Directors shall be held at the corporate offices, or such other place as may be designated by the Board of Directors, as follows:

Time of Regular Meeting: ______________________________

Date of Regular Meeting: ______________________________

If said day shall fall upon a holiday, such meetings shall be held on the next succeeding business day thereafter. No notice need to be given of such regular meetings.

Section 10. Special Meetings—Notices—Waivers. Special meetings of the Board may be called at any time by the Chairman of the Board or the President or any Vice President or the Secretary or any two (2) Directors (or one (1) Director if there is only one (1) Director).

If the notice is delivered personally to the Directors or personally communicated to them by a corporate Officer by telephone or telegraph, it shall be sent at least forty-eight (48) hours, or as required by state statute, prior to the meeting and such notice shall include the time and place of the meeting. If the notice is mailed to a Director by letter, it shall be addressed to him or her at his or her address as it is shown upon the records of the Corporation, or if it is not so shown on such records or is not readily ascertainable, at the place in which the meetings of the Directors are regularly held. In case such notice is mailed, it shall be deposited in the United States mail, postage prepaid, in the place in which the principal executive Officer of the Corporation is located at least five (5) days, or as required by state statute, prior to the time of the holding of the meeting. Such mailing, telegraphing, telephoning or delivery as above provided shall be due, legal and personal notice to such Director.

When all of the Directors are present at any Directors' meeting, however called or noticed, and either (i) sign a written consent thereto on the records of such meeting, or (ii) if a majority of the Directors are present and if those not present sign a waiver of notice of such meeting or a consent to whether prior to or after the holding of such meeting, which said waiver, consent or approval shall be filed with the Secretary of the Corporation, or (iii) if a Director attends a meeting without notice but without protesting, prior thereto or at its commencement, the lack of notice, then the transactions thereof are as valid as if had at a meeting regularly called and noticed.

The person or persons authorized to call special meetings of the Board of Directors may fix any place as the place for holding any special meeting of the Board of Directors called by them.

Section 11. Sole Director Provided by Articles of Incorporation or Bylaws. In the event only one (1) Director is required by the Bylaws or Articles of Incorporation, then any reference herein to notices, waivers, consents, meetings or other actions by a majority or quorum of the Directors shall be deemed to refer to such notice, waiver, etc., by such sole Director, who shall have all the rights and duties and shall be entitled to exercise all of the powers and shall assume all the responsibilities otherwise herein described as given to a Board of Directors.

Section 12. Entry of Notice. An entry in the minutes of any meeting of the Board of Directors to the effect that notice has been duly given shall be prima facie evidence that due notice of such special meeting was given to all Directors as required by laws and by these Bylaws.

Section 13. Waiver of Consent or Notice. The transactions at any meeting of the Board of Directors, however called or noticed, or wherever held, shall be as valid as if held after proper call and notice, if a quorum is present and, either before or after the meeting, each absent Director signs either a written waiver or notice, a consent to holding the meeting, or an approval of its minutes. These waivers, consents, and approvals shall be filed with the corporate records or made part of the minutes of the meeting. Neither the business to be transacted at, nor the purpose of, any regular or special Board meeting need be specified in the notice or waiver of notice of the meeting.

Attendance of a Director at any meeting shall constitute a waiver of notice of that meeting, unless a Director attends for the express purpose of objecting to the transaction of any business because the meeting is not properly called, noticed, or convened; provided, however, that if after stating his objection, the objecting Director continues to attend and by his attendance participates in any matters other than those objected to, he shall be considered to have waived notice of the meeting and withdrawn his objections.

Section 14. Action Without Meeting. The Board of Directors may take any action without a meeting that may be required or permitted to be taken by the Board at a meeting, if all members of the Board individually or collectively consent in writing to the action. The written consent or consents shall be filed in the minutes of the proceedings of the Board. The action by written consent shall have the same effect as a unanimous vote of Directors. Any certificate or other document filed with the minutes of the proceedings shall state that the action was taken by unanimous written consent of the Board without a meeting and that the Bylaws of the Corporation authorize this action.

Section 15. Quorum. A majority of the number of Directors as fixed by the Articles of Incorporation or Bylaws shall be necessary to constitute a quorum for the transaction of business, and the action of a majority of the Directors present at any meeting at which there is a quorum, when duly assembled, is valid as a corporate act; provided that a minority of the Directors, in the absence of a quorum, may adjourn from time to time, but may not transact any business. A meeting at which quorum is initially present may continue to transact business, notwithstanding the withdrawal of Directors, if any action taken is approved by a majority of the required quorum for such meeting.

Section 16. Adjournment. A quorum of the Directors may adjourn any Directors' meeting to meet again at a stated day and hour; provided, however, that in the absence of a quorum, a majority of the Directors present at any Directors' meeting, either regular or special, may adjourn from time to time until the time fixed for the next regular meeting of the Board.

Notice of the time and place of holding an adjourned meeting need not be given to absent Directors if the time and place are fixed at the meeting being adjourned.

Section 17. Fees and Compensation. Directors may receive a stated salary for their services as Directors or, by resolution of the Board, a fixed fee, which may or may not include expenses of attendance. Nothing herein contained shall be construed to preclude any Director from serving the Corporation in any other capacity as an Officer, agent, employee or otherwise, and receiving compensation therefor.

Section 18. Indemnity of Directors, Officers, and Employees. Every person who serves as a Director, Officer, or employee of the Corporation, and every person who serves at the written request of the Corporation (or at its oral request subsequently confirmed in writing) as a Director, Officer, or employee of another business, whether or not incorporated, in which the Corporation owns capital stock or other proprietary interests, or of which the Corporation is a creditor, may in the discretion of the Board of Directors be indemnified and held harmless by the Corporation from and against any loss, cost, liability, or expense that may be imposed on or incurred by him or her in connection with or resulting from any claim, action, suit, or proceeding, civil or criminal, in which he may become a party or otherwise be involved because of his being or having been a Director, Officer, or employee of the Corporation, or of any other business in which the Corporation may own capital stock or other proprietary interest, or of which the Corporation is a creditor, whether or not he has this relationship when the loss, cost, liability, or expense was imposed or incurred.

The phrase "loss, cost, liability or expense" shall include all expenses incurred in defense of the claim, action, suit, or proceeding and the amounts of judgments, fines, or penalties levied or rendered against the indemnified person, provided that no person shall be entitled to indemnity under this Section unless the Board of Directors determine in good faith that he was acting in good faith and within what he reasonably believed to be the scope of his employment or authority and for a purpose that he reasonably believed to be in the Corporation's or shareholders' best interests.

Payments authorized under this Section shall include amounts paid and expenses incurred in settling the claim, action, suit, or proceeding whether actually begun or only threatened. Expenses incurred with respect to a claim, action, suit, or proceeding indemnified against under this Section may be advanced by the Corporation before final disposition of the matter on receipt of an undertaking by or on behalf of the recipient to repay this amount if it is ultimately determined that he is not entitled to indemnification. This undertaking shall be satisfactory in form and amount to the Board of Directors.

This Section does not apply those expenses incurred by a party in any action instituted or maintained in the right of the Corporation by a shareholder or holder of a voting trust certificate representing shares of the Corporation.

Section 19. LIABILITY INSURANCE FOR DIRECTORS, OFFICERS AND EMPLOYEES. The Board of Directors may authorize the Corporation to pay, in whole or in part, the premium or other charge for any type of indemnity insurance in which any Officer, Director, or employee of the Corporation or any of its subsidiary Corporations is indemnified or insured against liability or loss arising out of his actual or asserted misfeasance or nonfeasance in the performance of his duties or out of any actual or asserted wrongful act against, or by, any of such Corporations including, but not limited to, judgments, fines, settlements and expenses incurred in the defense of actions, proceedings and appeals therefrom.

Section 20. COMMITTEES. Committees of the Board may be appointed by resolution passed by a majority of the whole Board. Committees shall be composed of two (2) or more members of the Board, and shall have such powers of the Board as may be expressly delegated to it by resolution of the Board of Directors as permitted by state law.

Section 21. ADVISORY DIRECTORS. The Board of Directors from time to time may elect one or more persons to be Advisory Directors who shall not by such appointment be members of the Board of Directors. Advisory Directors shall be available from time to time to perform special assignments specified by the President, to attend meetings of the Board of Directors upon invitation and to furnish consultation to the Board. The period during which the title shall be held may be prescribed by the Board of Directors. If no period is prescribed, the title shall be held at the pleasure of the Board.

ARTICLE IV
OFFICERS

Section 1. OFFICERS. The Officers of the Corporation shall be a President, a Secretary, and a Chief Financial Officer. The Corporation may also have, at the discretion of the Board of Directors, a Chairman of the Board, one or more Vice Presidents, one or more assistant secretaries, one or more assistant Treasurers, and such other Officers as may be appointed in accordance with the provisions of Section 3 of this Article IV. Any number of offices may be held by the same person.

Section 2. ELECTION. The Officers of the Corporation, except such Officers as may be appointed in accordance with the provisions of Section 3 or Section 5 of this Article, shall be chosen annually by the Board of Directors, and each shall hold office until he or she shall resign or shall be removed or otherwise disqualified to serve, or a successor shall be elected and qualified.

Section 3. Subordinate Officers. The Board of Directors may appoint, and empower the President to appoint, such other Officers as the business of the Corporation may require, each of whom shall hold office for such period, have such authority and perform such duties as are provided in the Bylaws or as the Board of Directors may from time to time determine.

Section 4. Removal and Resignation of Officers. Subject to the rights, if any, of an Officer under any contract of employment, any Officer may be removed, either with or without cause, by the Board of Directors, at any regular or special meeting to the Board, or, except in case of an Officer chosen by the Board of Directors, by any Officer upon whom such power of removal may be conferred by the Board of Directors.

Any Officer may resign at any time by giving written notice to the Board of Directors or the President or Secretary of the Corporation. Any such resignation shall take effect at the date of the receipt of that notice or at any later time specified in that notice; and, unless otherwise specified in that notice, the acceptance of the resignation shall not be necessary to make it effective. Any resignation is without prejudice to the rights, if any, of the Corporation under any contract to which the Officer is a party.

Section 5. Vacancies. A vacancy in any office because of death, resignation, removal, disqualification or any other cause shall be filled in the manner prescribed in the Bylaws for regular appointments to that office.

Section 6. Chairman of the Board. The Board of Directors may in its discretion elect a Chairman of the Board who shall, if present, preside at meetings of the Board of Directors and exercise and perform such other powers and duties as may be from time to time assigned by the Board of Directors or prescribed by the Bylaws. If there is no President, the Chairman of the Board shall in addition be the Chief Executive Officer of the Corporation and shall have the powers and duties prescribed in Section 7 of this Article IV.

Section 7. President. Subject to any supervisory powers that may be given by the Board of Directors or these Bylaws to the Chairman of the Board, or to an Officer senior to the President, if there be such an Officer, the President shall be the Corporation's Chief Executive Officer and shall, subject to the control of the Board of Directors, have general supervision, direction, and control over the Corporation's business and Officers. He or she shall preside as Chairman at all shareholders' meetings and at all Directors' meetings not presided over by the Chairman of the Board or by another senior Officer, if there be one. He or she shall be ex-officio a member of all the standing committees, including the executive committee, if any; shall have the general powers and duties of management usually vested in a Corporation's President; shall have any other powers and duties that are prescribed by the Board of Directors or these Bylaws; and shall be primarily responsible for carrying out all orders and resolutions of the Board of Directors. He or she may sign, with the Secretary or any other proper Officer of the Corporation thereunto authorized by the Board of Directors, certificates for shares of the Corporation, any deeds, mortgages, bonds, contracts, or other instruments which the Board of Directors has authorized to be executed, except in cases where the signing and execution thereof shall be expressly delegated by the Board of Directors or by these Bylaws to some other Officer or agent of the Corporation, or shall be required by law to be otherwise signed or executed.

Section 8. VICE PRESIDENT. In the absence or disability of the President, the Vice Presidents, if any, in order of their rank as fixed by the Board of Directors, or if not ranked, the Vice President designated by the Board of Directors, shall perform all the duties of the President, and when so acting shall have all the powers of, and be subject to, all the restrictions upon, the President. The Vice Presidents shall have such other powers and perform such other duties as from time to time may be prescribed for them respectively by the Board of Directors or the Bylaws.

Section 9. SECRETARY. The Secretary shall keep, or cause to be kept, a book of minutes at the principal office or such other place as the Board of Directors may order, of all meetings of Directors and shareholders, with the time and place of holding, whether regular or special, and if special, how authorized, the notice therof given, the names of those present at Directors' meetings, the number of shares present or represented at shareholders' meetings and the proceedings thereof.

The Secretary shall keep, or cause to be kept, at the principal office or at the office of the Corporation's transfer agent, a share register, or duplicate share register, showing the names of the shareholders and their addresses; the number and classes of shares held by each; the number and date of certificates issued for the same; and the number and date of cancellation of every certificate surrendered for cancellation.

The Secretary shall give, or cause to be given, notice of all the meetings of the shareholders and of the Board of Directors required by the Bylaws or by law to be given. He or she shall keep the seal of the Corporation in safe custody and shall have such other powers and perform such other duties as may be prescribed by the Board of Directors or by the Bylaws.

Section 10. CHIEF FINANCIAL OFFICER. The Chief Financial Officer shall keep and maintain, or cause to be kept and maintained in accordance with generally accepted accounting principles, adequate and correct accounts of the properties and business transactions of the Corporation, including accounts of its assets, liabilities, receipts, disbursements, gains, losses, capital, earnings (or surplus) and shares. The books of account shall at all reasonable times be open to inspection by any Director.

This Officer shall deposit all monies and other valuables in the name and to the credit of the Corporation with such depositories as may be designated by the Board of Directors. He or she shall disburse the funds of the Corporation as may be ordered by the Board of Directors, shall render to the President and Directors, whenever they request it, an account of all of his or her transactions and of the financial condition of the Corporation, and shall have such other powers and perform such other duties as may be prescribed by the Board of Directors or the Bylaws.

If required by the Board of Directors, this Officer shall give the Corporation a bond in the amount and with the surety or sureties specified by the Board for faithful performance of the duties of his office and for restoration to the Corporation of all its books, papers, vouchers, money, and other property of every kind in his possession or under his control on his death, resignation, retirement, or removal from office.

Section 11. Salaries. The salaries of the Officers shall be fixed from time to time by the Board of Directors and no Officer shall be prevented from receiving such salary by reason of the fact that he is also a Director of the Corporation.

Article V
Stock Certificates and Related Matters

Section 1. Stock Certificates. Certificates for shares shall be of such form and device as the Board of Directors may designate and shall state the following: (a) the name of the record holder of the shares represented thereby, (b) its number, (c) date of issuance, (d) the number of shares for which it is issued, (e) a statement of the rights, privileges, preferences and restrictions, if any, (f) a statement as to the redemption or conversion, if any; (g) a statement of liens or restrictions upon transfer or voting, if any; (h) if the shares be assessable or, if assessments are collectible by personal action, a plain statement of such facts.

One or more certificates for shares of the Corporation's capital stock shall be issued to each shareholder for any of his shares that are fully paid up. The corporate seal or its facsimile may be fixed on certificates.

All certificates shall be signed in the name of the Corporation by the Chairman of the Board or Vice Chairman of the Board or the President or Vice President and by the Chief Financial Officer or an Assistant Treasurer or the Secretary or any Assistant Secretary, certifying the number of shares and the class or series of shares owned by the shareholder.

Any or all of the signatures on the certificate may be facsimile. Every certificate authenticated by a facsimile of a signature must, before issuance, be countersigned by the signature or facsimile of the signature of a transfer agent or transfer clerk, and registered by an incorporated bank or trust company, either domestic or foreign, as registrar of transfers. A certificate authenticated by the signature, or facsimile signature of an Officer who by death, resignation, or otherwise has ceased to be an Officer of the Corporation before the certificate is delivered by the Corporation, shall be as valid as though signed by a duly elected, qualified and authorized Officer, if it is countersigned by the signature or facsimile of the signature of a transfer agent or transfer clerk and registered by an incorporated bank or trust company as registrar of transfers.

Section 2. Transfer of Stock. Shares of the capital stock of the Corporation may be transferred by endorsement and delivery of the certificate issued thereof at any time by the holder thereof in person or by an attorney legally constituted. The personal representative of any deceased stockholder and the guardian of any minor or incompetent may transfer the shares constituting a part of the estate subject to his control as provided by law. No transfer shall be valid until the surrender of the certificate and the acknowledgment of such transfer on the books of the Corporation. No new certificate shall be issued by the Secretary until a certificate for a corresponding number of shares has been surrendered for cancellation, and the Secretary shall cancel the surrendered certificate and preserve it as a voucher.

Section 3. LOST OR DESTROYED CERTIFICATES. Any person claiming a certificate of stock to be lost, destroyed, stolen or mutilated shall make an affidavit or affirmation of the fact and shall, if the Directors so require, give the Corporation a bond of indemnity, in the form and with one or more sureties satisfactory to the Board, in at least double the value of the stock represented by said certificate, and/or supply other appropriate protection by the person claiming same, whereupon a new certificate may be issued in the same tenor and for the same number of shares as the one alleged to be lost or destroyed.

Section 4. TRANSFER AGENTS AND REGISTRARS. The Board of Directors may appoint one or more transfer agents or transfer clerks, and one or more registrars, which shall be an incorporated bank or trust company, either domestic or foreign, who shall be appointed at such times and places as the requirements of the Corporation may necessitate and the Board of Directors may designate.

Section 5. RECORD DATE AND CLOSING STOCK BONDS. The Board of Directors may fix a time in the future, as a record date for the determination of the shareholders entitled to notice of or to vote at any meeting of shareholders, or entitled to receive any dividend or distribution, or any allotment of rights, or to exercise rights in respect to any change, conversion, or exchange of shares. The record date so fixed shall not be more than fifty (50) days prior to the date of the meeting or event for the purposes for which it is fixed. When a record date is so fixed, only shareholders of record on that date shall be entitled to notice of and to vote at the meeting, or to receive the dividend, distribution or allotment of rights, or to exercise the rights, as the case may be, notwithstanding any transfer of any shares on the books of the Corporation after the record date. The Board of Directors may close the books of the Corporation against transfers of shares during the whole or any part of any such fifty (50) day period.

If no record date is fixed, the record date for determining shareholders entitled to notice of or to vote at a meeting of shareholders shall be at the close of business on the business day next preceding the day on which notice is give, or, if notice is waived, at the close of business on the business day next preceding the day on which the meeting is held. The record date for determining shareholders entitled to give consent to corporate action in writing without a meeting, when no prior action by the Board is necessary, shall be the day on which the first written consent is given.

The record date for determining shareholders for any other purpose shall be at the close of business on the day on which the Board adopts the resolution relating thereto, or the fiftieth (50th) day prior to the date of such other action, whichever is later.

Section 6. LEGEND CONDITION. In the event any shares of this Corporation are issued pursuant to a permit or exemption therefrom requiring the imposition of a legend condition, the person or persons issuing or transferring said shares shall make sure said legend appears on the certificate and shall not be required to transfer any shares free of such legend unless an amendment to such permit or a new permit be first issued so authorizing such a deletion.

Section 7. Representation of Shares of Other Corporations. The President or any Vice President and the Secretary or any Assistant Secretary of this Corporation is authorized to vote, represent and exercise on behalf of this Corporation all rights incident to any and all shares of any other Corporation. The authority herein granted to said Officers to vote or represent on behalf of this Corporation any and all shares held by this Corporation in any other Corporation or Corporations may be exercised either by such Officers in person or by any persons authorized to do so by proxy or power of attorney duly executed by said Officers.

Article VI
Share Restrictions

Section 1. Provision Restricting Transfer of Shares. Before there can be a valid sale or transfer of any of the shares of this Corporation by the holders thereof, the holder of the shares to be sold or transferred shall first give notice in writing to the Secretary of this Corporation of his or her intention to sell or transfer such shares. Said notice shall specify the number of shares to be sold or transferred, the price per share and the terms upon which such holder intends to make such sale or transfer.

In the event that the consideration to be received by the transferor is other than cash, the notice shall fully describe such consideration and state the fair market value thereof. The Corporation, at its option and at the transferor's expense, may require the transferor to have the fair market value of such consideration determined by an independent appraiser selected by the Corporation. In the case of a non-cash consideration, the price per share shall be based upon the fair market value of the consideration as stated in the notice, unless the Corporation exercises its option to require the aforementioned independent appraisal, in which case the price per share shall be based upon such independently appraised fair market value.

The following are the only sales or transfers excluded from the provisions of this Article: Transfer by bequest, intestate succession, or gift to the spouse, lineal descendants, or adopted children, or to the spouses or adopted children of the lineal descendants, of the holder of the shares to be transferred, or to any custodian or trustee for the account of such persons. A sale or transfer which is so excluded from the provisions of this Article shall not remove those shares so transferred from the restrictions contained herein and any subsequent sale or transfer shall be subject to, and comply in all respects with said restrictions.

The Corporation shall have the prior right to purchase the shares referred to in the notice at the price and upon the terms and conditions stated in the notice. The Corporation may elect to purchase any portion or all of the shares referred to in the notice at the price and upon the terms and conditions stated therein.

If none or only a portion of the shares referred to in the notice are elected to be purchased by the Corporation in the foregoing manner, the shareholders who were holders of record of the Corporation on the date the notice was received by the Secretary of the Corporation shall have the right to purchase the shares referred to in the notice which the Corporation has not elected to purchase at the price and upon the terms and conditions stated in the notice and in accordance with the following provisions:

The Secretary shall within five (5) days thereafter, mail or deliver a copy of said notice to each of the other shareholders of record of this Corporation. Such notice may be delivered to such shareholders personally or may be mailed to the last known addresses of such shareholders, as the same may appear on the books of this Corporation. Within thirty (30) days after the mailing or delivery of said notices to such shareholders, any such shareholder or shareholders desiring to acquire any part or all of the shares referred to in said notice shall deliver by mail or otherwise to the Secretary of this Corporation a written offer or offers to purchase a specified number or numbers of such shares at the price and upon the terms stated in said notice.

If the total number of shares specified in such offers exceeds the number of shares referred to in said notice, each offering shareholder shall be entitled to purchase such proportion of the shares referred to in said notice to the Secretary, as the number of shares of this Corporation, which he or she holds bears to the total number of shares held by all shareholders desiring to purchase the shares referred to in said notice to the Secretary.

If all of the shares referred to in said notice to the Secretary are not disposed of under such apportionment, each shareholder desiring to purchase shares in a number in excess of his or her proportionate share, as provided above, shall be entitled to purchase such proportion of those shares which remain thus undisposed of, as the total number of shares which he or she holds bears to the total number of shares held by all of the shareholders desiring to purchase shares in excess of those to which they are entitled under such apportionment.

After receipt of all shareholder offers, to the extent that all of the shares referred to in the transferor's notice and statement are not disposed of under the preceding provisions, the Corporation shall have the right to increase the number of said shares it has elected to purchase.

Within forty (40) days after the notice is mailed or delivered to the Secretary, the Corporation shall deliver, by mail or otherwise, to the shareholder giving such notice a written statement of the number of shares referred to in the notice which the Corporation and/or the shareholders have elected to purchase.

The aforesaid right to purchase the shares referred to in the aforesaid notice to the Secretary shall apply only if all of the shares referred to in said notice are purchased. Unless all of the shares referred to in said notice to the Secretary are purchased, as aforesaid, in accordance with offers made within said forty (40) days, the shareholder desiring to sell or transfer may dispose of all shares of stock referred to in said notice to the Secretary to any person or persons whomsoever; provided, however, that he or she shall not sell or transfer such shares at a lower price or on terms more favorable to the purchaser or transferee than those specified in said notice to the Secretary.

Any sale or transfer, or purported sale or transfer, of the shares of said Corporation shall be null and void unless the terms, conditions and provisions of this section are strictly observed and followed.

Section 2. Pledged or Hypothecated Shares. Any shareholder desiring to borrow money on or hypothecate any or all of the shares of stock held by such shareholder shall first mail notice in writing to the Secretary of this Corporation of his or her intention to do so. Said notice shall specify the number of shares to be pledged or hypothecated, the amount to be borrowed per share, the terms, rate of interest, and other provisions upon which each shareholder intends to make such loan or hypothecation. The Secretary shall, within five (5) days thereafter, mail or deliver a copy of said notice to each of the other shareholders of record of this Corporation. Such notice may be delivered to such shareholder personally, or may be mailed to the last known addresses of such shareholders as the same may appear on the books of this Corporation. Within fifteen (15) days after the mailing or delivering of said notice to said shareholders, any such shareholder or shareholders desiring to lend any part or all of the amount sought to be borrowed, as set forth in said notice, at the terms therein specified, shall deliver by mail, or otherwise, to the Secretary of this Corporation a written offer or offers to lend a certain amount of money for the term, at the rate of interest, and upon the other provisions specified in said notice.

If the total amount of money subscribed in such offers exceeds the amount sought to be borrowed, specified in said notice, each offering shareholder shall be entitled to lend such proportion of the amount sought to be borrowed, as set forth in said notice, as the number of shares which he or she holds bears to the total number of shares held by all such shareholders desiring to lend all or part of the amount specified in said notice.

If the entire amount of monies sought to be borrowed, as specified in said notice, is not subscribed as set forth in the preceding paragraphs, each shareholder desiring to lend an amount in excess of his or her proportionate share, as specified in the preceding paragraph, shall be entitled to lend such proportion of the subscribed amount as the total number of shares which he or she holds bears to the total number of shares held by all of the shareholders desiring to lend an amount in excess of that to which they are entitled under such apportionment. If there be but one shareholder so desiring to lend, such shareholder shall be entitled to lend up to the full amount sought to be borrowed.

If none, or only a part of the amount sought to be borrowed, as specified in said notice, is subscribed as aforesaid, in accordance with offers made within said fifteen (15) day period, the shareholder desiring to borrow may borrow from any person or persons he or she may so desire as to any or all shares of stock held by him or her which have not been covered by lending shareholders; provided, however, that said shareholders shall not borrow any lesser amount, or any amount on terms less favorable to the borrower, than those specified in said notice to the Secretary.

Any pledge or hypothecation, or other purported transfer as security for a loan of the shares of this Corporation, shall be null and void unless the terms, conditions and provisions of these Bylaws are strictly observed and followed.

ARTICLE VII
RECORDS—REPORTS—INSPECTION

Section 1. **RECORDS.** The Corporation shall maintain, in accordance with generally accepted accounting principles, adequate and correct accounts, books and records of its business and properties. All of such books, records and accounts shall be kept at its principal executive office as fixed by the Board of Directors from time to time.

Section 2. **INSPECTION OF CORPORATE RECORDS.** The share register or duplicate share register, books of account, and minutes of proceedings of the shareholders', Directors', and committees of the Directors' meetings, including the executive committee meetings, shall be open to inspection on the written demand of any shareholder or holder of a voting trust certificate, at any reasonable time for a purpose reasonably related to his or her interests as a shareholder or voting trust certificate holder. These records shall further be exhibited at any time on the demand of the holders of ten percent (10%) of the shares represented at any shareholders' meeting. Any inspection under this Section may be made in person or by an agent or attorney, and shall include the right to make extracts. Demands to inspect, except at shareholders' meetings, shall be made in writing to the President, Secretary or Assistant Secretary of the Corporation.

Section 3. **CERTIFICATION AND INSPECTION OF BYLAWS.** The original or a copy of these Bylaws, as amended or otherwise altered to date, certified by the Secretary, shall be kept at the Corporation's principal executive office and shall be open to inspection by the shareholders of the Corporation at all reasonable times during office hours.

Section 4. **CHECKS, DRAFTS, ETC.** All checks, drafts or other orders for payment of money, notes or other evidences of indebtedness, issued in the name of or payable to the Corporation, shall be signed or endorsed by such person or persons and in such manner as shall be determined from time to time by resolution of the Board of Directors.

Section 5. **CONTRACTS, ETC.—HOW EXECUTED.** The Board of Directors, except as in the Bylaws otherwise provided, may authorize any Officer or Officers, agent or agents, to enter into any contract or execute any instrument in the name of and on behalf of the Corporation. Such authority may be general or confined to specific instances. Unless so authorized by the Board of Directors, no Officer, agent or employee shall have any power or authority to bind the Corporation by any contract or agreement, or to pledge its credit, or to render it liable for any purpose or to any amount, except as provided by law.

ARTICLE VIII
ANNUAL REPORTS

Section 1. **REPORT TO SHAREHOLDERS, DUE DATE.** The Board of Directors shall cause an annual report to be sent to the shareholders not later than one hundred twenty (120) days after the close of the fiscal or calendar year adopted by the Corporation. This report shall be sent at least fifteen (15) days before the annual meeting of shareholders to be held during the next fiscal year and in the manner specified in these Bylaws for giving notice to shareholders of the Corporation. The annual report shall contain a balance sheet as of the end of the fiscal year and an income statement and statement of changes in financial position for the fiscal year, accompanied by any report of independent accountants or, if there is no such report, the certificate of an authorized Officer of the Corporation that the statements were prepared without audit from the books and records of the Corporation.

Section 2. Waiver. The annual report to shareholders referred to in Article VIII, Section 1, is expressly dispensed with so long as this Corporation shall have less than one hundred (100) shareholders. However, nothing herein shall be interpreted as prohibiting the Board of Directors from issuing annual or other periodic reports to the shareholders of the Corporation as they consider appropriate.

Article IX
Amendments

Section 1. Amendments by Shareholders. New Bylaws may be adopted or these Bylaws may be amended or repealed by the persons entitled to vote a majority of the Corporation's voting shares, or their proxies, or by the written assent of these persons, except as otherwise provided by law or the Articles of Incorporation.

Section 2. Amendments by Directors. Subject to the right of shareholders as provided in Article IX, Section 1 above, to adopt, amend, or repeal Bylaws, Bylaws may be adopted, amended, or repealed by the Board of Directors; provided, however, that no Bylaws shall be adopted by the Directors which shall require more than a majority of the voting shares for a quorum at a meeting of shareholders, or more than a majority of the votes cast to constitute action by the shareholders, except where higher percentages are required by law or by the Articles of Incorporation.

Section 3. Record of Amendments. Whenever an amendment or new Bylaw is adopted, it shall be copied in the book of Bylaws with the original Bylaws, in the appropriate place. If any Bylaw is repealed, the fact of repeal with the date of the meeting at which the repeal was enacted or written assent was filed shall be stated in said book.

ARTICLE X
CORPORATE SEAL

The seal of the Corporation shall be circular in form and bear the name of the Corporation, the year of its organization and the words "CORPORATE SEAL, STATE OF ______________________________." The seal may be used by causing it to be impressed directly on the instrument or writing to be sealed, or upon adhesive substance affixed thereto. The seal on the certificates for shares or on any corporate obligation for the payment of money may be facsimile, engraved or printed.

ARTICLE XI
MISCELLANEOUS

Section 1. ACCOUNTING YEAR. The accounting year of the Corporation shall be fixed by resolution of the Board of Directors.

Section 2. CONSTRUCTION. Whenever a conflict arises between the language of these Bylaws and the Certificate of Incorporation, the Certificate of Incorporation shall govern.

CERTIFICATE OF ADOPTION OF BYLAWS

ADOPTION OF INCORPORATOR.

The undersigned person named in the Articles of Incorporation as the Incorporator of the above named Corporation hereby adopts the same as the Bylaws of said Corporation.

Executed this ________ day of ___________________________, 199 .]

____

Name

CERTIFICATE BY SECRETARY.

THIS IS TO CERTIFY:

That I am the duly elected, qualified and acting Secretary of the above named Corporation, that the foregoing Bylaws were adopted as the Bylaws of said Corporation on the date set forth above by the person named in the Articles of Incorporation as the Incorporator of said Corporation.

IN WITNESS WHEREOF, I have hereunto set my hand and affixed the corporate seal this ________ day of ___________________________, 199 .

____

Secretary

CERTIFICATE BY SECRETARY OF ADOPTION BY SHAREHOLDERS' VOTE.

THIS IS TO CERTIFY:

That I am the duly elected, qualified and acting Secretary of the above named Corporation and that the above and foregoing Code of Bylaws was submitted to the shareholders at their first meeting and recorded in the minutes thereof, was ratified by the vote of shareholders entitled to exercise the majority of the voting power of said Corporation.

IN WITNESS WHEREOF, I have hereunto set my hand this ________ day of ___________________________, 199 .

____

Secretary

Form **SS-4**
(Rev. April 1991)
Department of the Treasury
Internal Revenue Service

Application for Employer Identification Number

(For use by employers and others. Please read the attached instructions before completing this form.)

EIN

OMB No. 1545-0003
Expires 4-30-94

Please type or print clearly.

1 Name of applicant (True legal name) (See instructions.)

2 Trade name of business, if different from name in line 1

3 Executor, trustee, "care of" name

4a Mailing address (street address) (room, apt., or suite no.)

5a Address of business (See instructions.)

4b City, state, and ZIP code

5b City, state, and ZIP code

6 County and state where principal business is located

7 Name of principal officer, grantor, or general partner (See instructions.) ▶

8a Type of entity (Check only one box.) (See instructions.)
- ☐ Estate
- ☐ Trust
- ☐ Individual SSN ______
- ☐ Plan administrator SSN ______
- ☐ Partnership
- ☐ REMIC
- ☐ Personal service corp.
- ☐ Other corporation (specify) ______
- ☐ Farmers' cooperative
- ☐ State/local government
- ☐ National guard
- ☐ Federal government/military
- ☐ Church or church controlled organization
- ☐ Other nonprofit organization (specify) ______ If nonprofit organization enter GEN (if applicable) ______
- ☐ Other (specify) ▶ ______

8b If a corporation, give name of foreign country (if applicable) or state in the U.S. where incorporated ▶ | Foreign country | State

9 Reason for applying (Check only one box.)
- ☐ Changed type of organization (specify) ▶ ______
- ☐ Started new business
- ☐ Purchased going business
- ☐ Hired employees
- ☐ Created a trust (specify) ▶ ______
- ☐ Created a pension plan (specify type) ▶ ______
- ☐ Banking purpose (specify) ▶
- ☐ Other (specify) ▶

10 Date business started or acquired (Mo., day, year) (See instructions.)

11 Enter closing month of accounting year. (See instructions.)

12 First date wages or annuities were paid or will be paid (Mo., day, year). **Note:** *If applicant is a withholding agent, enter date income will first be paid to nonresident alien. (Mo., day, year)* . . . . ▶

13 Enter highest number of employees expected in the next 12 months. **Note:** *If the applicant does not expect to have any employees during the period, enter "0."* . . . . ▶	Nonagricultural	Agricultural	Household

14 Principal activity (See instructions.) ▶

15 Is the principal business activity manufacturing? . . . . ☐ Yes ☐ No
If "Yes," principal product and raw material used ▶

16 To whom are most of the products or services sold? Please check the appropriate box. ☐ Business (wholesale)
☐ Public (retail) ☐ Other (specify) ▶ ☐ N/A

17a Has the applicant ever applied for an identification number for this or any other business? . . . . ☐ Yes ☐ No
Note: *If "Yes," please complete lines 17b and 17c.*

17b If you checked the "Yes" box in line 17a, give applicant's true name and trade name, if different than name shown on prior application.

True name ▶ Trade name ▶

17c Enter approximate date, city, and state where the application was filed and the previous employer identification number if known.

Approximate date when filed (Mo., day, year)	City and state where filed	Previous EIN

Under penalties of perjury, I declare that I have examined this application, and to the best of my knowledge and belief, it is true, correct, and complete. | Telephone number (include area code)

Name and title (Please type or print clearly.) ▶

Signature ▶ Date ▶

Note: *Do not write below this line. For official use only.*

Please leave blank ▶	Geo.	Ind.	Class	Size	Reason for applying

For Paperwork Reduction Act Notice, see attached instructions. Cat. No. 16055N Form **SS-4** (Rev. 4-91)

Form **2553** (Rev. December 1990) Department of the Treasury Internal Revenue Service

Election by a Small Business Corporation

(Under section 1362 of the Internal Revenue Code)
▶ For Paperwork Reduction Act Notice, see page 1 of instructions.
▶ See separate instructions.

OMB No. 1545-0146
Expires 11-30-93

Notes: 1. *This election, to be treated as an "S corporation," can be accepted only if all the tests in General Instruction B are met; all signatures in Parts I and III are originals (no photocopies); and the exact name and address of the corporation and other required form information are provided.*

2. *Do not file Form 1120S until you are notified that your election is accepted. See General Instruction E.*

Part I Election Information

Please Type or Print

Name of corporation (see instructions)	A **Employer identification number** (see instructions)
Number, street, and room or suite no. (If a P.O. box, see instructions.)	B Name and telephone number (including area code) of corporate officer or legal representative who may be called for information
City or town, state, and ZIP code	C Election is to be effective for tax year beginning (month, day, year)

D Is the corporation the outgrowth or continuation of any form of predecessor? . . ☐ **Yes** ☐ **No**
If "Yes," state name of predecessor, type of organization, and period of its existence ▶ ....

E Date of incorporation

F Check here ▶ ☐ if the corporation has changed its name or address since applying for the employer identification number shown in item A above.

G State of incorporation

H If this election takes effect for the first tax year the corporation exists, enter month, day, and year of the **earliest** of the following: (1) date the corporation first had shareholders, (2) date the corporation first had assets, or (3) date the corporation began doing business. ▶

I Selected tax year: Annual return will be filed for tax year ending (month and day) ▶ ....
If the tax year ends on any date other than December 31, except for an automatic 52-53-week tax year ending with reference to the month of December, you **must** complete Part II on the back. If the date you enter is the ending date of an automatic 52-53-week tax year, write "52-53-week year" to the right of the date. See Temporary Regulations section 1.441-2T(e)(3).

J Name of each shareholder, person having a community property interest in the corporation's stock, and each tenant in common, joint tenant, and tenant by the entirety. (A husband and wife (and their estates) are counted as one shareholder in determining the number of shareholders without regard to the manner in which the stock is owned.)	K Shareholders' Consent Statement. We, the undersigned shareholders, consent to the corporation's election to be treated as an "S corporation" under section 1362(a). (Shareholders sign and date below.)*		L Stock owned		M Social security number or employer identification number (see instructions)	N Shareholder's tax year ends (month and day)
	Signature	Date	Number of shares	Dates acquired		

*For this election to be valid, the consent of each shareholder, person having a community property interest in the corporation's stock, and each tenant in common, joint tenant, and tenant by the entirety must either appear above or be attached to this form. (See instructions for Column K if continuation sheet or a separate consent statement is needed.)

Under penalties of perjury, I declare that I have examined this election, including accompanying schedules and statements, and to the best of my knowledge and belief, it is true, correct, and complete.

Signature of officer ▶ **Title ▶** **Date ▶**

See Parts II and III on back. Form **2553** (Rev. 12-90)

Form 2553 (Rev. 12-90) Page 2

Part II Selection of Fiscal Tax Year (All corporations using this Part must complete item O and one of items P, Q, or R.)

O Check the applicable box below to indicate whether the corporation is:

1. ☐ A new corporation adopting the tax year entered in item I, Part I.
2. ☐ An existing corporation retaining the tax year entered in item I, Part I.
3. ☐ An existing corporation changing to the tax year entered in item I, Part I.

P Complete item P if the corporation is using the expeditious approval provisions of Revenue Procedure 87-32, 1987-2 C.B. 396, to request: **(1)** a natural business year (as defined in section 4.01(1) of Rev. Proc. 87-32), or **(2)** a year that satisfies the ownership tax year test in section 4.01(2) of Rev. Proc. 87-32. Check the applicable box below to indicate the representation statement the corporation is making as required under section 4 of Rev. Proc. 87-32.

1. Natural Business Year ▶ ☐ I represent that the corporation is retaining or changing to a tax year that coincides with its natural business year as defined in section 4.01(1) of Rev. Proc. 87-32 and as verified by its satisfaction of the requirements of section 4.02(1) of Rev. Proc. 87-32. In addition, if the corporation is changing to a natural business year as defined in section 4.01(1), I further represent that such tax year results in less deferral of income to the owners than the corporation's present tax year. I also represent that the corporation is not described in section 3.01(2) of Rev. Proc. 87-32. (See instructions for additional information that must be attached.)

2. Ownership Tax Year ▶ ☐ I represent that shareholders holding more than half of the shares of the stock (as of the first day of the tax year to which the request relates) of the corporation have the same tax year or are concurrently changing to the tax year that the corporation adopts, retains, or changes to per item I, Part I. I also represent that the corporation is not described in section 3.01(2) of Rev. Proc. 87-32.

Note: *If you do not use item P and the corporation wants a fiscal tax year, complete either item Q or R below. Item Q is used to request a fiscal tax year based on a business purpose and to make a back-up section 444 election. Item R is used to make a regular section 444 election.*

Q Business Purpose—To request a fiscal tax year based on a business purpose, you must check box Q1 and pay a user fee. See instructions for details. You may also check box Q2 and/or box Q3.

1. Check here ▶ ☐ if the fiscal year entered in item I, Part I, is requested under the provisions of section 6.03 of Rev. Proc. 87-32. Attach to Form 2553 a statement showing the business purpose for the requested fiscal year. See instructions for additional information that must be attached.

2. Check here ▶ ☐ to show that the corporation intends to make a back-up section 444 election in the event the corporation's business purpose request is not approved by the IRS. (See instructions for more information.)

3. Check here ▶ ☐ to show that the corporation agrees to adopt or change to a tax year ending December 31 if necessary for the IRS to accept this election for S corporation status in the event: (1) the corporation's business purpose request is not approved and the corporation makes a back-up section 444 election, but is ultimately not qualified to make a section 444 election, or (2) the corporation's business purpose request is not approved and the corporation did not make a back-up section 444 election.

R Section 444 Election—To make a section 444 election, you must check box R1 and you may also check box R2.

1. Check here ▶ ☐ to show the corporation will make, if qualified, a section 444 election to have the fiscal tax year shown in item I, Part I. To make the election, you must complete **Form 8716,** Election To Have a Tax Year Other Than a Required Tax Year, and either attach it to Form 2553 or file it separately.

2. Check here ▶ ☐ to show that the corporation agrees to adopt or change to a tax year ending December 31 if necessary for the IRS to accept this election for S corporation status in the event the corporation is ultimately not qualified to make a section 444 election.

Part III Qualified Subchapter S Trust (QSST) Election Under Section 1361(d)(2)**

Income beneficiary's name and address	Social security number
Trust's name and address	Employer identification number

Date on which stock of the corporation was transferred to the trust (month, day, year) ▶

In order for the trust named above to be a QSST and thus a qualifying shareholder of the S corporation for which this Form 2553 is filed, I hereby make the election under section 1361(d)(2). Under penalties of perjury, I certify that the trust meets the definition requirements of section 1361(d)(3) and that all other information provided in Part III is true, correct, and complete.

Signature of income beneficiary or signature and title of legal representative or other qualified person making the election — Date

**Use of Part III to make the QSST election may be made only if stock of the corporation has been transferred to the trust on or before the date on which the corporation makes its election to be an S corporation. The QSST election must be made and filed separately if stock of the corporation is transferred to the trust after the date on which the corporation makes the S election.

*U.S. GPO:1991-518-943/20365

APPENDIX TWO

Recommended Resources

HELP IS ONLY A PHONE CALL AWAY!

Important Numbers

- Federal Information Center/800-347-1997
- Internal Revenue Service/800-829-1040
- American Association of Home Based Businesses/ 202-310-3130
- Small Business Administration/800-U-ASK-SBA
- World Information Link/800-841-4441
- International Trade Administration/800-USA-TRADE
- International Franchise Administration/202-659-0790
- National Association of Women Business Owners/ 312-922-0465
- Department of Commerce/800-347-1997
- The Business Source, Inc.—Business Development and Training—703-255-3133

Books, Tapes and Software References

Marketing Boot Camp—85 Profit Packed Tips, Techniques & Strategies to Boost Your Bottom Line Now, Sanow/McComas, Dubuque, IA, Kendall/Hunt Publishing, 1994, $29.95, 800-228-0810.

The Corporation Manual—An unequalled guide to using corporations for tax savings, protection and wealth building. Jerry Perone, $64.95, 301-590-0710.

Working Solo: The Real Guide To Freedom and Financial Success With Your Own Business. New Paltz, NY, Portico Press, 1994, $14.95.

How To Run A Small Business, 7th Edition, New York, McGraw-Hill 1994, $27.95.

The Entrepreneur's Guide To Preparing A Winning Business Plan and Raising Venture Capital, Englewood Cliffs, NJ, Prentice Hall, 1990, $28.95.

Creating Effective Boards for Private Enterprise, Josey-Bass, 1991, $25.95.

Cash Flow Problem Solver, Bryan Milling Sourcebooks, 1992, $19.95.

Quick-Books by Intuit, small business bookkeeping/accounting software.

THE CENSUS BUREAU

A Very Important Source Of Information

(All Numbers are 301 area code unless indicated otherwise)

CENSUS CUSTOMER SERVICES
(Data product and ordering information for computer tapes, CD-ROMs, microfiche and some publications) 763-4100 FAX 763-4794

➪ Agriculture Information	1-800-523-3215
➪ Business Information	763-1792
➪ Census Job Information (Recording)	763-6064
➪ Census Personnel Locator	763-7662
➪ Congressional Affairs	763-2446
➪ Foreign Trade Information	763-5140/7754
➪ General Information	763-4100
➪ Library	763-5042
➪ Population Information	763-5002/5020 (TTY)
➪ Public Information Office (Press)	763-4040

CENSUS REGIONAL OFFICES
(Information services, data product information)

➪ Atlanta, GA	404-730-3833
➪ Boston, MA	617-565-7078
➪ Charlotte, NC	704-344-6144

➪ Chicago, IL	312-353-0980
➪ Dallas, TX	214-767-7105
➪ Denver, CO	303-969-7750
➪ Detroit, MI	313-226-7742
➪ Kansas City, KS	913-236-3711
➪ Los Angeles, CA	818-904-6339
➪ New York, NY	212-264-4730
➪ Philadelphia, PA	215-597-8313
➪ Seattle, WA	206-728-5314
➪ Regional Office Liaison	202-763-4683

CENSUS BUREAU KEY CONTACTS

Access to Census Records (Age Search)	812-285-5314
Bulletin Board—Nancy Smith	763-1580
CENDATA (Online Service)	763-2074
Census & You (Newsletter)—Neil Tillman	763-1584
Census History—Frederick Bohme	763-7936
County & City, State & Metropolitan Area Data Books—Wanda Cevis	763-1034
Factfinders (General information booklets)—Frederick Bohme	763-7936
Historical Statistics	763-1034
Microdata Files—Carmen Campbell	763-2005
Statistical Abstract—Glenn King	763-5299
Statistical Briefs—Robert Bernstein	763-1584
Statistical Research:	
Demographic—Lawrence Ernst	763-7880
Economic—C. Easley Hoy	763-5702
1990 Census Tabulations & Publications—	
U.S.: Gloria Porter	763-3938
Puerto Rico & Outlying Areas—Lourdes Flaim	763-2903

CENSUS BUREAU SUBJECT MATTER EXPERTS

Agriculture

Agriculture & Crop Statistics—Donald Jahnke	763-8567
Data Requirements & Outreach—Douglas Miller	763-8561
Farm Economics—James Liefer	763-8514
General Information—Tom Manning	1-800-523-3215
Irrigation & Horticulture Statistics—John Blackledge	763-8559
Livestock Statistics—Linda Hutton	763-8569

Demographics & Population

Aging Population, U.S.—Arnold Goldstein	763-7883
Ancestry—Susan Lapham	763-7955
Apportionment—Robert Speaker	763-7962
Child Care—Martin O'Connell/Amara Bachu	763-5303/4547
Children—Donald Hernandez	763-7987
Citizenship—Susan Lapham	763-7955
Commuting, Means of Transportation, & Place of Work—Phil Salopek/Celia Boertlein	763-3850
Crime—Gail Hoff	763-1735

Geographic

Annexations, Boundary Changes—Nancy Goodman	763-3827
Area Measurement—Jim Davis	763-3827
Census Geographic Concepts	763-3827
Census Tracts—Cathy Miller	763-3827
Centers of Population—Jim Davis	763-3827
Congressional Districts:	
Address Allocations	763-5692
Boundaries, Component Areas—Cathy McCully	763-3827
Fee-Paid Block Splits—Joel Miller	763-3827
State Boundary Certification—Louise Stewart	763-3827

Housing

American Housing Survey—Edward Montfort	763-8551
Census—Bill Downs	763-8553
Communications & Utilities Census—Dennis Shoemaker	763-2662
Construction Building Permits—Linda Hoyle	763-7244
Construction in MSAs—Joseph Gilvary	763-7842
Finance, Insurance, & Real Estate Census—Sidney Marcus	763-5718
Housing Starts & Completions—David Fondelier	763-5731
Market Absorption/Residential Finance—Anne Smoler/Peter Fronczek	763-8165
New York City Housing & Vacancy Survey—Margaret Harper	763-8171
Residential Characteristics, Price Index, Sales—Steve Berman	763-7842
Residential Improvements & Repairs—George Roff	763-5705
Vacancy Data—Wallace Fraser/Robert Callis	763-8165
Value of New Construction—Allan Meyer	763-5717

Income, Poverty, & Wealth

Consumer Expenditure Survey—Ron Dopkowski	763-2063
Household Wealth—T. J. Eller	763-8578
Income Statistics	763-8576
Poverty Statistics	763-8578

International Statistics

Africa, Asia, Latin America, North America, & Oceania—Frank Hobbs	763-4221
Aging Population—Kevin Kinsella	763-4884
China, People's Republic—Loraine West	763-4012
Europe—Godfrey Baldwin	763-4020
Former Soviet Union—Marc Rubin	763-4020
Health—Karen Stanecki	763-4086

International Data Base—Peter Johnson 763-4811

Women in Development—Patricia Rowe 763-4221

Labor Force

Commuting, Means of Transportation, & Place of Work—Phil Salopek/Celia Boertlein 763-3850

Employment & Unemployment—Thomas Palumbo/Selwyn Jones 763-8574

Journey to Work—Phil Salopek/Gloria Swieczkowski 763-3850

Occupation & Industry Statistics 763-8574

Maps

Computer Mapping—Fred Broome 763-3973

1980 Census Map Orders—Ann Devore 812-288-3192

1990 Census Maps 763-4100

Metropolitan Areas—James Fitzsimmons 763-5158

Outlying Areas—Virgeline Davis 763-3827

Urban/Rural Residence—Robert Speaker 763-7962

Urbanized Areas & Urban/Rural Concepts—Nancy Torrieri 763-3827

User-Defined Areas Program (Neighborhood Statistics)—Adrienne Quasney 763-4282

Voting Districts—Cathy McCully 763-3827

ZIP Codes:

Demographic Data 763-4100

Economic Data—Anne Russell 763-7038

Nondurables

Census & Annual Survey—Michael Zampogna 763-2510

Current Industrial Reports—Judy Dodds 763-5911

Population Survey

General Information 763-4100

Disability—Jack McNeil/Bob Bennefield 763-8300/8578

Education 763-1154

Equal Employment Opportunity Data—Tom Scopp	763-8199
Fertility & Births—Martin O'Connell/Amara Bachu	763-5303/4547
Foreign Born	763-7955
Group Quarters Population—Denise Smith	763-2784
Health Surveys—Robert Mangold	763-5684
Hispanic & Ethnic Statistics	763-7955
Homeless—Annetta Clark	763-2784
Household Estimates	763-5002
Households & Families—Steve Rawlings	763-7987
Immigration: Legal—Susan Lapham	763-7955
Undocumented & Emigration—Edward Fernandez	763-5590
Journey to Work—Phil Salopek/Gloria Swieczkowski	763-3850
Marital Status & Living Arrangements—Arlene Saluter	763-7987
Metropolitan Areas (MAs):	
Population—POP	763-5002
Standards—James Fitzsimmons	763-5158
Migration—Kristen Hansen/Diana DeAre	763-3850
National Estimates & Projections	763-5002
Outlying Areas—Michael Levin	763-5134
Place of Birth—Kristin Hansen	763-3850
Population Information	763-5002/5020 (TTY)
Prisoner Surveys—Gail Hoff	763-1735
Puerto Rico—Lourdes Flaim	763-2903
Race Statistics	763-2607/7572
Reapportionment & Redistricting—Marshall Turner, Jr.	763-3856
State & County Estimates	763-5002
State Projections	763-5002
Travel Surveys—John Cannon	763-5468
Women—Denise Smith	763-2784

Retail Trade	
Advance Monthly—Ronald Piencykoski	763-5294
Census—Anne Russell	763-7038
Monthly Report—Irving True	763-7128
Services	
Census—Jack Moody	763-7039
Current Reports—Thomas Zabelsky	763-5528
Special Topics	
Business Owners—Eddie Salyers	763-5470
Census Products—Paul Zeisset	763-1792
County Business Patterns—Zigmund Decker	763-5430
Enterprise Statistics—Eddie Salyers	763-5470
Industry & Commodity Classification—James Kristoff	763-1935
Investment in Plant & Equipment—John Gates	763-5596
Mineral Industries—John McNamee	763-5938
Minority- & Women-Owned Businesses—Eddie Salyers	763-5470
Puerto Rico & Outlying Areas—Kent Hoover	763-8559/8564
Quarterly Financial Report—Paul Zarrett	763-2718
Transportation	
Census—Dennis Shoemaker	763-2662
Commodity Flow Survey—John Fowler	763-6087
Truck Inventory and Use—Bill Bostic	763-2735
Warehousing & Trucking—Tom Zabelsky	763-5528
Wholesale Trade	
Census—John Trimble	763-5281
Current Sales & Inventories—Nancy Piesto	763-3916

U.S. SMALL BUSINESS ADMINISTRATION (SBA)
Established To Help You Be Successful

The Small Business Administration

The SBA offers an extensive selection of information on most business management topics, from how to start a business to exporting your products. This information is listed in The Small Business Directory. For a free copy write to:

SBA Publications
P.O. Box 1000
Fort Worth, TX 76119

The SBA has offices throughout the country. The SBA offers a number of programs and services, including training and educational programs, counseling services, financial programs and contract assistance. You should consult the U.S. Government section in your telephone directory for the office nearest you.

Ask about:

- Service Corps of Retired Executives (SCORE), a national organization sponsored by SBA of over 13,000 volunteer business executives who provide free counseling, workshops and seminars to prospective and existing small business people.
- Small Business Development Centers (SBDCs), sponsored by the SBA in partnership with state and local governments, the educational community and the private sector. They provide assistance, counseling and training to prospective and existing business people.
- Small Business Institutes (SBI), organized through SBA on more than 500 college campuses nationwide. The institutes provide counseling by students and faculty to small business clients.

For more information about SBA business development programs and services, call the SBA Small Business Answer Desk at 1-800-U-ASK-SBA (827-5722).

Other U.S. Government Resources

Many publications on business management and other related topics are available from the Government Printing Office (GPO). GPO bookstores are located in 24 major cities and listed in the Yellow Pages under the "bookstore" heading. You can request a subject bibliography by writing to Government Printing Office, Superintendent of Documents, Washington, DC 20402-9328.

Many federal agencies offer publications of interest to small businesses. There is a nominal fee for some, but most are free. Below is a selected list of government agencies that provide publications and other services targeted to small businesses. To get their publications, contact the regional offices listed in the telephone directory or write to the addresses below:

Consumer Information Center (CIC)
P.O. Box 100
Pueblo, CO 81002

Consumer Product Safety Commission (CPSC)
Publications Request
Washington, DC 20207

U.S. Department of Agriculture (USDA)
12th Street and Independence Avenue, SW
Washington, DC 20250

U.S. Department of Commerce (DOC)
Office of Business Liaison
14th Street and Constitution Avenue, NW
Room 5898C
Washington, DC 20230

U.S. Department of Health and Human Services
Public Health Service
Alcohol, Drug Abuse and Mental Health Administration
5600 Fishers Lane
Rockville, MD 20857

U.S. Department of Labor (DOL)
Employment Standards Administration
200 Constitution Avenue, NW
Washington, DC 20210

Drug Free Workplace Helpline: 800-843-4971. Provides information on Employee Assistance Programs.

National Institute for Drug Abuse Hotline: 800-662-4357. Provides information on preventing substance abuse in the workplace.

The National Clearinghouse for Alcohol and Drug Information: 1-800-729-6686 toll-free. Provides pamphlets and resource materials on substance abuse.

U.S. Department of Treasury
Internal Revenue Service (IRS)
P.O. Box 25866
Richmond, VA 23260
1-800-424-3676

U.S. Environmental Protection Agency
Small Business Ombudsman
Cystal Mall—No.2
Room 1102
1921 Jefferson Davis Highway
Arlington, VA 22202
1-800-368-5888 except in DC and VA
703-557-1938 in DC and VA

U.S. Food and Drug Administration (FDA)
FDA Center for Food Safety and Applied Nutrition
200 C Street, SW
Washington, DC 20204

For More Information Consult The Library

A librarian can help you locate the specific information you need in reference books. Most libraries have a variety of directories, indexes and encyclopedias that cover many business topics. They also have other resources, such as:

- **Trade Association Information.** Ask the librarian to show you a directory of trade associations. Associations provide a valuable network of resources to their members through publications and services such as newsletters, conferences and seminars.
- **Books**. Many guidebooks, textbooks and manuals on small business are published annually. To find the names of books not in your local library, check "Books In Print," a directory of books currently available from publishers.
- **Magazine and Newspaper Articles.** Business and professional magazines provide information that is more current than that found in books and textbooks. There are a number of indexes to help you find specific articles in periodicals.
- **Free Workshops and Seminars.** Many libraries offer free workshops, lend skill-building tapes and have catalogues and brochures describing continuing education opportunities.

SBA Loan Programs

The SBA is Congressionally mandated to assist the nation's small businesses in meeting their financing needs. This is accomplished primarily through SBA's 7(a) loan program, the Certified Development Company (503/504) loan program; and the Small Business Investment Company (SBIC) program. In addition, the SBA now administers the Microloan Demonstration Program. These many and varied programs are described below.

1. The 7(a) Loan Program

The 7(a) Loan Program is the largest of the SBA's financial assistance programs, constituting over 80% of all SBA business lending activity. This program includes three types of loans; Guaranteed, Direct and Immediate Participation loans.

Guaranteed Loans. Guaranteed Loans are made and disbursed by private lenders and guaranteed by SBA. If a borrower defaults on a guaranteed loan, SBA will purchase an agreed upon percentage of the unpaid balance. By law, SBA can guaranty a maximum of $500,000.

- *Contract Loan Program.* The Contract Loan Program is a short-term line of credit designed to finance the estimated costs of labor and materials needed to perform a specific contract. The loans are guaranteed by the SBA and do not allow revolving account access to funds guaranteed by the agency. These loans are available only under SBA's guaranty program. Eligible businesses may have more than one contract loan outstanding at any given time as long as SBA's total exposure does not exceed $750,000.
- *Seasonal Line of Credit Program.* The Seasonal Line of Credit Program offers short-term loans to help small businesses get past cash crunches attributable to seasonal changes in business volume. The loans are guaranteed by the SBA and are used to finance increases in trading assets, such as receivables and inventory, required as a result of seasonal upswings in business. These loans are available only under the guaranty loan program.
- *Export Revolving Line of Credit Loan Program.* The SBA's Export Revolving Line of Credit Program (ERLC) is designed to help small businesses obtain short-term financing to sell their products and services abroad. The program guarantees repayment to a lender in the event an exporter defaults. By reducing a lender's risks, the ERLC provides an incentive for lenders to finance small business exporters working capital needs. The ERLC protects only the lender from default by the exporter; it does not cover the exporter should a foreign buyer default on payment. Lenders and exporters must determine whether foreign receivables need credit risk protection.
- *Small General Contractor Loans.* The SBA makes regular business loans to small general contractors to finance construction or renovation of residential or commercial buildings that will be offered for sale. These loans are available only under the guaranty loan program.

- *International Trade Loan Program.* The International Trade Loan Program helps small businesses that are engaged or preparing to engage in international trade, as well as small businesses adversely affected by competition from imports. Loans are made by lending institutions with the SBA guaranteeing a portion of the loan.

Loans not exceeding $155,000: SBA may guaranty up to 90% of all loans under $155,000 except where loan proceeds will be used to refinance existing debt, in which case SBA's guaranty maximum is 80%.

Loans exceeding $155,000: SBA can guaranty a maximum of 85% and a minimum of 70% of loans exceeding $155,000 except when part or all of the loan proceeds will be used to refinance existing debt, in which case the rules enumerated above apply. With new money having exposure to exceed $750,000 a lesser guaranty is permitted as long as SBA's exposure is limited to $750,000.

Direct Loans. Direct Loans are available only to borrowers who are unable to obtain lender participation loans. Although the legal ceiling on direct loans is $350,000, SBA has set an administrative ceiling for these loans of $150,000. Direct loan applications in excess of $150,000 can only be accepted with the approval of the Regional Administrator. Because of present funding limitations, direct loans are available only to certain categories of borrowers. These include Vietnam-era and disabled veterans, the handicapped, low-income borrowers and businesses located in high unemployment areas. In order to establish that the requested financing is not otherwise available, a good faith attempt must be made to secure the requested financing from a private lender (from two lenders in cities of 200,000 people or more).

- *Veterans Loan Program.* Vietnam-era veterans and veterans with 30% or more disability are eligible for SBA's direct loan program as well as the guaranty program. Vietnam-era veterans are defined as veterans who served for a period of more than 180 days, any part of which was between August 5, 1964 and May 7, 1975, and who were discharged other than dishonorably. Disabled veterans are defined as veterans with a disability discharge or with a 30% or more compensable disability. To qualify, the eligible veteran must own at least 1% of the business and participate in its day-to-day activities. The credit criteria for veteran loans are the same as for all SBA borrowers.

- *7(a) 11 Loan Program.* Businesses located in high-unemployment or low-income areas, as well as businesses owned by low-income individuals, are eligible for SBA's direct loan program. To qualify, a business must be located in an area designated by the Department of Labor as having severe or persistent unemployment; or must be more than 50% owned by low-income individuals, defined for the purpose of this program as those individuals having inadequate income to meet basic family needs.
- *Handicapped Assistance Loans.* Disabled individuals and public or private non-profit organizations for the employment of the handicapped can get SBA financing for starting, acquiring or operating a small business. The loans are available under the Handicapped Assistance Loan Program.

Immediate Participation Loans. Immediate Participation Loans are those made jointly by SBA and private lenders whereby either SBA or the participating lender makes the loan, then, upon disbursement, the other participant immediately purchases its agreed upon share of the loan. These loans can be serviced either by the lender or by SBA. Immediate Participation loans are permissible subject to funding availability, only when a guaranty loan is unavailable. SBA's participation is limited to 75% or $150,000 whichever is less, except in cases where a participant's legal limit precludes a 25% participation.

Loan Provisions. In general, the following provisions apply to all SBA 7(a) loans. The special loan programs are enumerated later and, where necessary, special provisions are pointed out.

Small businesses which can meet SBA's size and policy standards are eligible for the 7(a) loan program. Ineligible businesses include those engaged in illegal gambling, speculation, media, lending, and real property for sale or investment (rental property). The specific terms of SBA loans are negotiated between an applicant and the participating financial institution in the case of guaranty and immediate participation loans, subject to the concurrence of SBA. SBA and the borrower negotiate the terms of direct loans, subject to SBA's policy and lending requirements.

The loan can be of any amount as long as the SBA-guaranteed portion of the loan (or combination of all outstanding loans to any one borrower) does not exceed $500,000. Direct loans (or a combination of all outstanding direct loans to any one borrower) cannot exceed $150,000 except when a waiver is obtained from the Regional Office in which case this maximum is $350,000.

Loan proceeds may be used to establish a new business or to assist in the operation, acquisition, or expansion of an existing business, including working capital; the purchase of inventory, machinery and equipment; and the construction, expansion and rehabilitation of business property.

2. Section 504 Certified Development Company Program

The SBA provides long-term financing to small businesses through its Certified Development Company Program. The program makes loans available for acquiring land, buildings, machinery and equipment, and for building, modernizing, renovating or restoring existing facilities and sites.

A certified development company (CDC) is a private, public sector non-profit corporation that is set up to contribute to the economic development of its community or region. It must:

- Operate in a defined area;
- Be composed of 25 or more members who are geographically representative of the CDC's area of operation and who include representatives from government agencies in the area of operation, private sector lending institutions, businesses and community organizations;
- Provide a full-time professional staff who can market the program and process, close and service its loan portfolio;
- Have the ability to sustain its operations on a continuous basis from reliable sources of funds;
- Have five or more directors who meet quarterly. At least one director must have commercial lending experience; and

- Have incorporated within its bylaws and articles that its chief purpose is to promote and assist the growth and development of business concerns in its operation area.

3. Micro Loan Program

The SBA started the Micro Loan Program to meet the ever-growing need for loans of $50,000 or less. These loans will be particularly valuable to small firms in the service sector.

A new and simplified application form (SBA Form 4 Short Form) has been designed by the SBA to make the program easier to use.

Under this program, the SBA changed the fee for guaranteeing the loans to participating lenders and simplified the application form to encourage lenders to consider SBA-guaranteed loans of $50,000 or less. The change in the program allows lenders making SBA-guaranteed loans of $50,000 or less with maturities greater than 12 months to retain half of the guarantee fee that is normally paid to the SBA. For example, a $50,000 loan with a 90% guarantee has an SBA-guaranteed portion of $45,000, and the 2% guarantee fee would be $900. Under the new changes, the lender may retain $450 and forward $450 to SBA or, at its option, the lender may choose not to charge the small business borrower the half of the guaranty that it would have retained.

APPENDIX THREE

Additional Resources and Services from the Authors

JERRY PERONE
SPEAKER—TRAINER—AUTHOR—CONSULTANT

Jerry Perone, MBA, is the president and founder of The National Management Center, Inc., a nationwide small business management and financial consulting firm. Jerry is one of America's leading authorities in directing and providing a broad array of services aimed at helping entrepreneurs and individuals protect themselves and their families from financial loss due to business reversals, changes in the marketplace, lawsuits, income taxes, and other devastating possibilities.

Jerry is known for his skills and abilities in communicating complex financial and tax concepts in a clear, easy to follow and entertaining style. He has consulted with many individuals, small-business operators and Fortune 500 companies, including IBM, Department of Commerce, Virginia Peninsula Chamber of Commerce, Merrill Lynch, American Express, NASD and Maglev, to name a few.

Jerry holds a number of seminars and conferences throughout the year focused on the profit, protection and planning needs of entrepreneurs, professionals and small-business operators.

Jerry's most requested topics include:

- *Take Your State Income Taxes to Zero*
- *How To Become Lawsuit Proof Forever*
- *Global Wealth Preservation*
- *How to Bulletproof Your Corporation*
- *How To Start Your Business With The Little Money You Have*
- *Corporate Owner's Workshop*
- *How To Choose The Right Business Form For You*
- *Keep It In The Family*
- *Tax and Strategy Workshop*
- *How To Implement an Error Free Investment Plan*

Jerry is a frequent guest on television, radio and in the print media. Recent appearances include "The Home Business Show" on the NETV-Metromedia and "It's Your Business" on WPGC radio. In addition, Jerry is an adjunct professor at Howard University. His next book, *Wealth: How To Make It, How To Keep It!* is due out in the winter of 1995.

Whether you're looking for a powerful keynote speaker, seminar and training programs or customized consultation, Jerry is the right choice.

For more information on making your next event a memorable one, call Jerry today!

The National Management Center, Inc., 301-590-0710

THE NATIONAL MANAGEMENT CENTER, INC.

6701 Democracy Boulevard, Suite 300
Bethesda, MD 20817
Phone 301-590-0710 Fax 301-590-0460

HOW WE CAN HELP YOU ACHIEVE YOUR GOALS

Innovation Evaluation	Designed to assist entrepreneurs in determining the market potential of ideas or innovations.
Corporate Officer and Secretary Services	Corporate officers can, in several situations, be held personally liable for business actions. To protect your family wealth and assist with your business development, we provide corporate officers and corporate secretary services.
Lawsuit and Asset Protection Planning	This is our specialty. We can erect a shield around your business and personal assets. Each year there are over 20,000,000 lawsuits filed in the U.S. Jury awards are skyrocketing. Don't get caught without a defense.
Business Structuring	Corporations, partnerships, limited liability companies —don't make the wrong choice. Lawyers do not always fully understand the business and tax issues. Accountants do not always know the strategies. We can help.
Tax Minimization Strategies	Taxes now consume almost 50% of your profits. We can show you how to use interstate business strategies to virtually eliminate state income taxes and substantially reduce federal income taxes.
Business Plans and Strategy	Comprehensive, insightful, detailed planning structured to help you achieve your goals and financial independence.
Management Systems	Leave no stone unturned. Customized management systems and procedures to match your personal leadership style and maintain the control you need.
Sales and Marketing Plans and Strategy	Unique sales and marketing approaches to sell your product or service in today's competitive, high tech world.
Marketing Research	In-depth market and competitive research to reduce risk, protect capital, and maximize your profits.
Financial Plans and Strategy	Sound financial plans to keep you afloat. Don't be short of funds. Know how much money you need to launch your business venture, how to get it and how to use it.
Employee Leasing	Don't let new healthcare programs threaten your profitability. We can restructure all of your current personnel, including you, into a money saving lease arrangement.
Individual Consultation	Whatever your needs, we'll be there. By the hour or under contract. We help you solve your problems—today!

MENU OF CORPORATE MANAGEMENT SERVICES

Professional Director Services

This service includes serving as an elected Director or officer for your corporation and the preparation and execution of up to 24 documents per year.

Corporate Secretary Services

This service includes serving as the secretary and maintaining the corporate kit, the corporate records and all formalities.

Basic Director Service

This service only includes serving as the Director or officer of your corporation, allowing you to keep your name off any public records.

Other Services

Complete Corporate Record Inspection
Federal Corporate Tax Returns
Miscellaneous Resolutions and Documents
Consulting
Corporate Catch-Up

THE NATIONAL MANAGEMENT CENTER, INC.

Phone: 301-590-0710

Menu of Educational Services

Product or Service	Media	Price
Rent-A-Mentor: Jerry Perone will serve as your personal and/or business financial mentor. With years of financial and business experience to draw upon, Jerry will be "at your side" to assist you in becoming your own financial and corporate expert.	Consulting Services	Individually Priced
Lawsuits & Asset Protection: Overview of the tools and techniques to protect your wealth and save taxes.	Audio Tape—1 hour live seminar from 1993 Paper Source Convention	$10.95
How to Structure Your Business and Financial Affairs: Explains step by step how to structure your financial affairs to reduce taxes and protect your assets.	Paperback book—45 pages Includes charts and diagrams	$29.95
The Corporation Manual: Explains everything you'll ever need to know about corporations in order to use them to their maximum.	Binder—over 200 pages Includes charts and diagrams	$64.95
Corporation Strategies: Explains many strategies that can be implemented to use corporations to eliminate state income taxes, achieve total financial privacy and much more.	Binder—over 50 pages Includes charts, diagrams and contacts	$39.95
How to Reduce Your Taxes Using Corporations: Presents and explains the basic income taxation for corporations and how to plan your expenditures to benefit fully.	Binder—over 50 pages Includes charts, tables and diagrams	$39.95
Corporate Forms and Resolutions: Contains a blank copy of all the forms, resolutions and minutes you'll ever need to prevent personal liability exposures.	Folder—over 50 forms All corporate forms, minutes and resolutions needed	$29.95
Marketing Boot Camp: An extraordinary book. Over 85 strategies that you can use today to get business to come to you.	Hardback book—over 175 pages	$29.95

ASK US TO TRAIN YOUR STAFF!

The National Management Center trains business people annually throughout the United States. We provide customized seminars tailored to your unique needs. Our clients seek The National Management Center for 1 hour, 1/2 day, full day, weekend retreats and long-term training agreements. Each National Management Center seminar is the result of months of intensive research, years of practical experience, and scores of interviews with those in the know. This information is then organized and presented to your company in a clear and concise "how to" format. If you would like additional information please feel free to call us at (301) 590-0710. Thank you.

Do It Yourself Marketing Research
How to Bullet Proof Your Corporation
Tax and Strategy Workshop for Small Business Owners
Corporate Owner's Workshop
How to Start Your Business With the Little Money That You Have
How to Become Lawsuit Proof Forever
Sole Proprietorships Versus Corporations—The End of the Debate
Finance for the Non-Financial Manager
Financial Skills for Salespeople
Financial Decision Making for Executives
Increased Profits Via Project Management
Project Management for Executives
Successful Management Strategies for the 90s
The Secrets of Breakthrough Planning

ARNOLD SANOW
SPEAKER—TRAINER—AUTHOR—CONSULTANT

Arnold Sanow, MBA, is one of America's leading authorities in the area of business development and personal effectiveness.

Whether you're looking for a powerful keynote, seminar or training program, Arnold is the right choice! His customized presentations are fast-paced, energetic, high-content and fun. But most of all, Arnold's sessions contain solid "how to" information that can be used immediately.

Arnold has given over **2,000 paid presentations and consults** with a variety of companies, associations and governmental organizations throughout the USA and overseas.

Arnold's speaking and training engagements have included such organizations as:

AT&T
C-SPAN
PBS
Intuit
National Association of Credit Management
American Red Cross
American University
U.S. Navy
U.S. Department of Commerce
National Glass Association
American Association of Art Museum Directors
National Solid Waste Management Association
Meeting Planners International
American Indian Heritage Foundation
SkillPath Seminars
Boston Society of Architects
Harvard Club
Health Management Associates
National Institutes of Health
National Homebuilders Association
National Office Machine Dealers Association
Delphi International
Czechoslavakian (Government)
World Trade Center of Trinidad and Tabago

AND MORE!

Arnold's most requested topics include:

- *Communicate Like a Pro*
- *How to Make Powerful Presentations*
- *How to Provide Exceptional Customer Service*
- *Marketing Professional Services*
- *Marketing & Publicity on a Low Budget*
- *Skills for Success*
- *No Time to Kill . . . Managing Multiple Priorities*
- *Managing and Leading People*
- *Secrets of Successful Entrepreneurs*
- *How to Become a Successful Consultant and Speaker*

Arnold is a frequent guest on radio, television and in the print media. He is the author of the best-selling books, **"You Can Start Your Own Business"** and **"Marketing Boot Camp"** and has been featured on such shows as the **CBS Evening News with Dan Rather,** *USA Today, Entrepreneur Magazine* and others. He is a regular columnist for the *Washington Business Advisor* and former talk show host of the radio show, "It's Your Business." Arnold is an adjunct professor at Georgetown University and President of The Business Source, Inc., a Business Development and Training Company.

Arnold lives in Vienna, Virginia with his wife Nancy and son, Stevie.

For more information on making your next event a memorable one, call Arnold today!

The Business Source, Inc., 703-255-3133

SERVICES & PRODUCTS FOR GROWING BUSINESSES

Arnold Sanow
THE BUSINESS SOURCE, INC.
703-255-3133

The Business Source, Inc., is your *"one stop"* Business Development and Training firm. Whether you're just starting, a one person business or a growing operation, we can assist you in determining practical solutions and developing the right strategies to help your company grow and prosper in this competitive environment.

MANAGEMENT AND MARKETING CONSULTING

The Business Source offers short and long term, "How To" practical advice on management, marketing, customer service, sales, planning and more. Perfect for start up's to those in the Fortune 500. We provide high quality, practical solutions to the critical questions that face companies like yours each and every day.

CUSTOMIZED TRAINING

Every year we train thousands of people from business, government, and associations throughout the USA and Overseas. We offer keynote, 1–3 hour, full day, weekend retreats, ongoing training programs and individual coaching sessions. Our programs include: *How to provide excellent customer service; Marketing professional services; Marketing and publicity on a low budget; Managing and leading people; Communicate like a pro; Skills for success; How to make powerful presentations; No time to kill . . . successful time management strategies; Entrepreneur boot camp; How to become a successful consultant; and Speak and grow rich.*

BUSINESS AND MARKETING PLANS

There are two reasons why you need a business and marketing plan. First, it is almost impossible to get financing without a plan; Second, you need it to effectively run your company. Whether your business is a start-up, an ongoing concern, or is in a turnaround situation, the time spent on planning can mean the difference between success and failure. If you need a few hours of consulting, a "skeleton plan" or a full blown plan, we can help!

BUSINESS PHYSICAL . . . ASSESSMENT/AUDIT

Every business needs a periodic check up to make sure it is running smoothly. Our assessment/audit includes analysis of the management, marketing, communication between internal and external customers, financial systems, computerization, personnel, and other functions necessary to the success of your business. A regular *"tune-up"* can alleviate problems before they start.

MARKETING RESEARCH

Do you have a clear picture of both your present and potential market? Failure to understand your market can be devastating. Lack of information about potential and current customers is often cited as the main reason for many business problems and failures. Through research techniques such as focus groups, surveys, mystery shopping, and others, we will help you to successfully target your customers.

BUYING OR SELLING A BUSINESS?

Whether you're looking for a business to buy, or you want to sell your business, we can help. We handle all details, develop a marketing plan, advertise, screen potential purchasers and help you get the most for your business. For interested buyers, we help you decide the best business to get into and then investigate the potential candidates.

SPEAKER/CONSULTANT MENTOR PROGRAM

According to Tony Robbins, "The best way to increase your chances of success is to have a mentor or a coach who is successful in the field you wish to get into." This unique one-on-one "fast start" mentoring/coaching program will help you set up your own speaking/consulting business on a part or full time basis. Arnold Sanow, who has been a successful speaker (presented over 2,000 paid presentations) and consultant for over 10 years will share with you the strategies and techniques that will save you money, time, frustration and help you avoid the mistakes that plague many consultants and speakers. In addition, Arnold will meet with you on an ongoing basis to make sure you're never alone! If you want to be your own boss, set up your own speaking or consulting business and learn the ABC's, this customized coaching is for you!

******ASK ABOUT OUR BOOKS, TAPES & EDUCATIONAL MATERIALS******
All titles available at between 20% to 50% off published price.

For More Information . . . Arnold Sanow
The Business Source, Inc.
703-255-3133

DO YOU NEED A SPEAKER OR TRAINER?

Invest in yourself, your people and your company.

The Business Source, Inc., has given over 2,000 customized seminars and training programs to organizations like yours. Our high-yield, step-by-step, nuts and bolts seminars are entertaining and informative! We offer a variety of programs, presented by our experts to become the "one stop" source for all your training needs. Whether you're looking for a 45 minute dinner speech, or a 1/2 day, full day, weekend retreat or long term training program, we can meet your needs.

Below is a list of our most popular topics. If you would like further information on how we can make your next meeting or training session memorable and productive please place an "X" next to the appropriate topic. Please send this form to the address below or call us at 703-255-3133 or fax this form to 703-255-4668. Thank you.

__ **The 5 Most Common Mistakes Managers Make . . . And How To Avoid Them**

__ **Marketing Boot Camp . . . Boost Your Bottom Line Now!**

__ **Communicate Like A Pro . . . And Win More Sales!**

__ **Success Skills**

__ **Keep Your Customers For Life . . . Effective Customer Service Strategies**

__ **No Time To Kill . . . Time Management Strategies**

__ **Entrepreneur Boot Camp**

__ **Leadership Skills For The 90's And Beyond**

__ **Present Like A Pro! . . . Presentation Skills Training**

__ **Speaking And Consulting For Big $$$$**

__ **Effective Team Building**

Name: ____

Address: ______________________________ Zip Code __________

Phone: Home ____________________ Business ____________________

Arnold Sanow
THE BUSINESS SOURCE, INC.
2810 Glade Vale Way
Vienna, Virginia 22181
703-255-3133

LEARN TO BECOME A HIGHLY PAID SPEAKER & CONSULTANT!

EARN UP TO $1,000 AND MORE FOR EACH PRESENTATION!

Jump-start your speaking and consulting career and earn up to $50 to $1,000 dollars an hour—and more.

The purpose of this customized one to one speaking/consulting training program is to help you break into the exciting world of being a paid professional speaker and consultant!

By becoming a paid professional speaker/consultant, you will:

- ***Be your own boss***
- ***Work when you want to***
- ***Control your own destiny***
- ***Gain more clients***
- ***Increase your current income***
- ***Become highly visible . . . Get the recognition you deserve***
- ***Develop a better social and professional life***
- ***Inspire others to change or improve their lives***

Hello, my name is Arnold Sanow. I have given over 2,000 paid presentations and consulted with hundreds of clients throughout the USA and Overseas. For nearly a decade, I have made my living by speaking and helping people like yourself to learn the ***"inside secrets"*** of the speaking and consulting business. To help you get on the ***"fast track,"*** I will work with you on a one to one basis. I will then customize a training program tailored to your unique needs. You will learn from my trials and tribulations exactly what you need to do to start and succeed in your own business. As your ***mentor*** and ***coach,*** I will save you time, money, frustration and help you avoid those costly mistakes that can ruin your business. ***In fact, you will acquire 10 years of experience in a very short time!***

I will design a customized marketing plan to help you:

- **Set up your own speaking and consulting business . . . step by step**
- **Determine the best direction for you to follow**
- **Learn how to market yourself**
- **Find the right contacts**
- **Know the right people and places to network your services**
- **Learn the best topics to speak on . . . and provide you with outlines**
- **Increase the level of your presentation skills**
- **Price your speaking engagements and consulting assignments**
- **Find all the resources you'll need to succeed**
- **Develop products and services to complement your seminar/consulting programs**
- **Know virtually everything it takes to succeed in your own business!**

To help your speaking business move in the right direction, I will work with you on an ***ongoing basis*** to make sure things happen . . . and ***you'll never be alone!*** As your personal manager, I will help you manage your new career. You'll receive:

- ***Meetings on a regular basis . . . You'll never be alone . . . No chance to procrastinate***
- ***Outlines . . . Complete scripts on topics of interest to you***
- ***Manual . . . My manual will provide you with virtually everything a successful speaker/consultant needs to know***
- ***Subcontracting possibilities***
- ***Networking on your behalf . . . We will work behind the scenes to sell your services***
- ***Media and Publicity Kit***
- ***Speaking/Consulting Opportunities***
- ***Help in becoming "famous"***
- ***Video and Live presentation skills training***
- ***Ghost-written articles available for your use at no additional charge***
- ***Books, Tapes and Other Services to sell at your seminars and training sessions***
- ***Learn how to get your own book published and earn extra $$$***

Plus Membership in my Speakers and Consultants Bureau . . . We will act as your agent

If you have ***always dreamed of being a well paid speaker/consultant;*** If you have always been thinking of ***developing your speaking/consulting potential*** and ***don't know how to get started;*** If you've been saying, I'm going to do this someday and ***never get around to it;*** If you don't have the ***time or interest in marketing yourself;*** If you ***don't know what to speak on,*** or your ***afraid of taking on this monumental task by yourself;*** Let me help you start on what could be the ***greatest adventure of your life!***

Please feel free to call me anytime so that we can discuss the fantastic possibilities that could change your life. My phone number is (703) 255-3133. Thank you.

P.S.—Unsolicited Testimonial from a recent client; Dear Arnold: "You are the best mentor an aspiring speaker and author could have discovered. Thanks to your guidance, this book is a reality and my law firm is growing everyday! Thank You . . . Thank You . . . Thank You . . ." Warmest Regards, Cheryl Frank.

ENTREPRENEUR BOOT CAMP

Customized . . . On Site Seminars

Arnold Sanow and Jerry Perone, authors of the critically acclaimed book *Entrepreneur Boot Camp* will provide your organization with a customized, step-by-step, nuts and bolts seminar tailored to your unique needs.

Great for companies downsizing, conventions, keynotes, for your clients and more!

All of your questions will be answered. Nothing will be held back!

Have you or your associates gone to a seminar, gotten all fired up and then didn't know where to start or simply lost your momentum? You'll find this is much, much more than "just a seminar." Everything you'll get is proven, tested information, not pie-in-the-sky theory. In this stimulating, thought-provoking day, we'll teach you practical strategies to increase your profits and cut your costs!

We'll help you identify your biggest (and immediate) profit and growth opportunities and show you how to effectively exploit them. No long winded theory here! Just fast-paced, "street smart," straight-to-the-point strategies that will increase your billings, fees, profits and customer loyalty.

Your *Entrepreneur Boot Camp* seminar will show you:

- ➩ The exact step-by-step strategy for setting up your business.
- ➩ The 12 characteristics and traits that most successful entrepreneurs share.
- ➩ Over 50 free and low-cost resources to assist your business.
- ➩ The five hottest businesses for the 90s that you can start for under $10,000.
- ➩ Five low-cost marketing strategies that will set your business on the fast track.
- ➩ How and where to get financing . . . plus little known, but effective resources.
- ➩ Different business structures to keep your taxes low!
- ➩ Business plan strategies that win $$$ . . . and keep your business on track.
- ➩ A roadmap toward your success.

and much, much more—including quick-read checklists to make sure you don't miss a step, sample forms, case studies, action plans and proven marketing documents you can use right away to jump-start your marketing efforts!

Call us now and let us show you how Arnold Sanow's and Jerry Perone's on-site seminar, *Entrepreneur Boot Camp,* will help you not only survive, but thrive!

National Management Center, Inc.
301-590-0710